DEAR CEO

DEAR CEO

50 Personal Letters from the World's Leading Business Thinkers

COMPILED BY
STUART CRAINER AND
DES DEARLOVE

Bloomsbury Business
An imprint of Bloomsbury Publishing Plc

BLOOMSBURY
LONDON • OXFORD • NEW YORK • NEW DELHI • SYDNEY

Bloomsbury Business
An imprint of Bloomsbury Publishing Plc

50 Bedford Square
London
WC1B 3DP
UK

1385 Broadway
New York
NY 10018
USA

www.bloomsbury.com

BLOOMSBURY and the Diana logo are trademarks of Bloomsbury Publishing Plc

First published 2017

British Library Cataloguing-in-Publication Data
A catalogue record for this book is available from the British Library.

ISBN: HB: 978-1-4729-5068-0
ePDF: 978-1-4729-5067-3
ePub: 978-1-4729-5069-7

Library of Congress Cataloging-in-Publication Data
A catalog record for this book is available from the Library of Congress.

Cover design by Eleanor Rose
Cover image © Getty Images

Typeset by Integra Software Services Pvt. Ltd.
Printed and bound in Great Britain

CONTENTS

FOREWORD

Bringing together letters from many interesting and thoughtful people – including university professors, writers, consultants and CEOs themselves – this really is a fascinating book! As a CEO myself, I am also one of the recipients.

The differences in the writers' backgrounds and positions mean that these letters are about very different things. For example, some raise the issue of care for female employees, while some urge the CEO to act on their commitments to consumers. Written by fifty top business thinkers from around the world, these letters touch on methodologies, theories, processes and results, as well as the journey to realizing personal dreams and goals. This book deserves to be called an encyclopaedia of ideas for CEOs.

A great Chinese scholar called Liang Shuming said that there are three cultures in the world: the Chinese culture focuses on relations between people; the Indian culture focuses on one's relation with oneself; and the Western culture is mainly about the relation between people and nature. From this perspective, these fifty letters can be read by any CEO, regardless of their cultural backgrounds. The ideas are universal and applicable to all CEOs, wherever they may be working.

My company, the Haier Group, is undergoing its own transformation, based on Internet management. Although there are many Internet technology companies in the world, few scholars and businesses have studied and implemented effective Internet management strategies. This is strikingly similar to the Industrial Revolution, which was triggered by inventions such as the steam engine but only blossomed following the introduction of assembly lines.

As part of the changes initiated by Haier, we are committed to giving everyone the chance to be their own CEO. This book should therefore enjoy a large and growing audience.

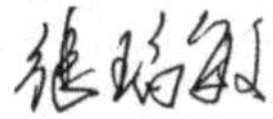

Zhang Ruimin
Chairman and CEO, Haier Group

Introduction

Midway through the Wimbledon Men's Singles Final the television cameras scanned the crowd in the royal box. There were past winners, sporting greats, politicians and celebrities of various degrees of permanence. Among them was a single figure who appeared less intent on the irresistible rise of Novak Djokovic and more on the smartphone in his hand. He was Sir Martin Sorrell, the CEO of WPP.

For the modern CEO there is no rest from the steady stream of emails, the demands on their time. There is no hiding place.

At the very top, there appears a relish for such demands. Sir Martin famously promises to reply to anyone in WPP who emails him within twenty-four hours. He calculates that for anyone to bother the CEO it has to be something important.

Talking with one CEO, he summed up his modus operandi: 'The reality is that every time I am on the move, I make a call; every time I have a break I call someone. I go through a mental list of who I haven't spoken to for a while or someone who I know has a new piece of work on, or family news – they've just had a new baby or something.'

And yet, here was a man clearly happy in his work. 'The life of a CEO is not for everyone', he told us. 'It is a gruelling, stressful and often lonely, existence. It is physically, mentally and emotionally demanding. And, of course, there is no guarantee of success or even survival in the post. So why do it? Because, on a good day, it is also the best job in the world.'

Most jobs come with a job description, a lengthy list of the exact parameters of responsibility. But when you reach corporate leadership roles, the job descriptions come to an end. You are left alone to make it up as you go along. The only sure thing is that you will be expected to deliver results.

The loneliness can be oppressive – and partly explains the rise of the executive coaching industry. Not knowing what it is you should do or when or with who offers more freedom than most executives have usually experienced in the corporate cocoon. In their previous incarnations executives have often been purveyors of certainty; as CEOs they find that uncertainty rules. It can bewilder even the best prepared.

Little coherent research has been done as to how executives do and should manage their daily working lives. Filling out a six-page academic survey is rarely high on a CEO's daily to-do list. Indeed, the reality largely went unexplored until Henry Mintzberg's *The Nature of Managerial Work*, published in 1973.

Instead of spending time contemplating the long term, Mintzberg found that managers were slaves to the moment, moving from task to task with every move dogged by another diversion, another call. The median time spent on any one issue was a mere nine minutes. Remember this was nearly a quarter of a century before email.

So, this is the world of the CEO: constant interruptions, seemingly impossible demands on your time, unable to confide in people, unsure who to trust, uncertain as to what you can and can't say.

What to do?
We asked a global selection of leading business thinkers what advice they would pass onto CEOs? What do CEOs really need to know and pay attention to?

Dear CEO is the result.
We believe it provides vital food for thought for anyone who is already a CEO and anyone who aspires to become a CEO. It is the leadership agenda for our turbulent times.

Stuart Crainer and Des Dearlove
Thinkers50 Founders

From Jamie Anderson and Ayelet Baron

Dear CEO,

When you were growing up many people told you to have big ambitions – to shoot for the moon. And congratulations – you have made it. Not only have you become a member of the 'C-Suite', as the CEO you have risen to a level of responsibility that most people only ever dream of. But maybe you are starting to question what success means to you, and to realize that you no longer want to be defined solely by what you do for a living. That this success that you have achieved, that this person that you have become, is not really what you want at all? So what should you do next?

Now, of course, many top executives define themselves with and through their work, and all other things in life are subordinate. If you are one of those executives, then you can stop reading now. But if you aspire to something more, to a wider definition of success, then please read on.

Since the inception of the industrial age, one of the pinnacles of success has been achieving the level of top management in a large organization. There has been an unwritten manual, leading from being a successful child to a teenager to an adult. It has included getting an education, an education that has opened the door to a good job, promotion and career. Along the way, you may or may not have been successful in finding a life partner and establishing a family, or to contributing to community in a wider sense. Much has depended on your perceived notion of personal, societal and material success.

In your current story of success, you have sometimes felt that you are two separate people – your professional self and personal self – and somehow you have been expected to balance those two distinct areas of your life. But maybe your successful career has meant a less successful life in a wider sense, as to climb the corporate ladder has meant that you have made many sacrifices.

An increasing number of people in the ranks of the C-Suite are questioning whose dream they have been living in an attempt to get back in touch with their own dreams and to engage with a wider and more human definition of success. So the first thing to do is to realize that you are not having some kind of midlife crisis – you are having a midlife reality check. And, of course, given that many of us will live beyond a century, this reality check can be coming in your fifties or beyond.

It is time for you to start creating purposeful goals that go beyond being recognized and generating value for the organization – these goals might relate to parenting, philanthropy, hobbies or even sporting ambitions. So you need to take some time out – some time to slow down and reflect. This rethinking of goals might not come quickly, and you might even experience a period where you lack direction, but that is to be expected after years or even decades on a linear career path.

And, of course, this process of rethinking goals should not be done alone – it should be done with those you love, and the goals that are created should be shared goals. You need to accept that life success is not about 'me' it is about 'us'. And after you have redrawn this picture of success, you need to ask if your current life as CEO is compatible. If it is not, then it is time to change. But we are not for a moment suggesting that this is about retirement – smart people can engage in a spectrum of work activities that still allow energy and time for other life goals.

If you decide to pursue a new path, there will be fears. The first set of fears will be deeply personal, related to worries about financial security or losing status or never being able to go back. The second set of fears you are likely to experience will relate to the social and professional environments in which you find yourself – the anxiety of letting people down. The reaction from some of these around you will be shock and disbelief, and in some cases even manifest itself in a sense of betrayal. But in the end, you must realize that not everyone will understand the decision of a non-linear career path choice. The people who matter the most are close friends and family – as they are the ones who need to have their own fears addressed.

What we are encouraging you to do is to embark on a way of living in which you, and not the organization, define the meaning of success. There is nothing wrong with career success – we are all for it. But the reality is that the responsibilities that accompany high achievement in most organizations place an overwhelming emphasis on loyalty to the institution ahead of wider life goals.

We wish you every 'success' in continuing to shoot for the moon. But there are many moons out there in the universe, so just make sure that the moon you are shooting for is your own.

Yours sincerely,

Jamie Anderson and Ayelet Baron

Jamie Anderson is a speaker, author and cyclist. He is co-author of *The Fine Art of Success* and creator of the popular TED talk 'What Is Success, Really?'.

Ayelet Baron (ayeletbaron.com) is an entrepreneur, speaker and author. She is a former Cisco executive, served as an Innovator in Residence at Roche/Genentech and is the author of *Our Journey to Corporate Sanity: Transformation Stories from the Frontiers of 21st Century Leadership* (Param Media, 2017).

From Scott Anthony

Conquering Increasing Uncertainty with Dual Transformation

Dear CEO,

It's cliché to say that the pace of change is accelerating. Indeed, that statement has arguably been true since the renaissance. But something feels different today. Businesses built painstakingly over decades get ripped apart almost overnight. Innosight's research shows that 50 per cent of the companies on the S&P 500 will not be on the list in ten years. Many of the companies that will replace today's giants likely do not even exist today.

Every business leader needs to think about the impact of ever-accelerating change. Broad trends such as the rise of robots and drones, the disappearance of computers into everyday life, everything-as-a-service and big data analytics promise to bring disruptive change to every nook and cranny of the global economy.

Many leaders describe increasing uncertainty as an existential challenge. Indeed, it causes a leader to question his or her very identity. Most leaders ascended to their current position by mastering the intricacies of today's business, making rigorous, fact-based decisions. They need to develop new skills to make decisions using judgement and intuition, replacing an optimization mindset with an exploration one.

While the pattern of market leaders being felled by disruptive upstarts feels like an essential factor of capitalism, it carries a heavy transaction tax, destroying know-how formulated over decades and ripping local communities apart. And, it is unnecessary, because the forces that threaten to disrupt today's business simultaneously creates the possibilities of creating tomorrow's. Leaders that learn how to bend the forces of disruption in their favour can own the future, rather than be disrupted by it.

Responding to the challenge requires executing what we call *dual transformation.* Transformation A repositions today's business to increase its relevance and resilience. Think about how Adobe shifted its core business from selling packaged software to providing on-demand access over the Internet, or Hilti went from selling tools to providing tool management solutions. Transformation B creates tomorrow's growth engine. Consider how Amazon.com turned an internal effort to accelerate IT projects into a multi-billion-dollar cloud computing offering, or how Nestlé is creating a portfolio of health and wellness businesses.

We call it *dual* transformation because these two transformations need to be pursued in parallel. This is not unrelated diversification. Rather, Transformations A and B should be connected by a carefully crafted and actively managed 'capabilities link' that flips the innovator's dilemma into an opportunity. After all, while a large company can't innovate *faster* than the market, it can innovate *better* than the market if it combines together unique assets of scale with entrepreneurial energy.

Dual transformation is the greatest challenge a leadership team will ever face. Successfully managed, it reconfigures the essence of a company. Some of the old remains, just as it does when a caterpillar becomes a butterfly or ice turns into steam. But, as in those metaphors, the form or substance of an organization fundamentally changes. Mastering dual transformation requires:

- The **courage to choose** before signals are clear. The more obvious the need to transform, paradoxically, the harder it is to do it.
- The **clarity to focus** on tomorrow's growth opportunities, even if it means saying goodbye to important pieces of yesterday's business.
- The **curiosity to explore** in the face of significant uncertainty, and to handle the inevitable false steps, fumbles and, yes, failures that comes along with moving in new directions.
- The **conviction to persevere** in the face of dark days, when key executives question the depth of commitment, conflict between today and tomorrow emerges and fundamental issues of identity threaten to distract or derail progress.

Dual transformation is also the greatest opportunity a leadership team will face. Disruptive change creates a window of opportunity to create massive new markets. It is the moment where the market also-ran can become the market leader. It is the moment when business legacies are created.

To start the journey of becoming the next version of yourself, ask three deceptively simple questions. Who are we today? Who will we become tomorrow? How do we start making the change? Remember that the biggest risk is not the action you take; it is trying fruitlessly to cling to the status quo as the world changes around you.

Leaders that catch disruptive changes early and respond appropriately will have the ability to thrive in the years to come. Those that don't, well, Darwin has a way of taking care of them.

Scott Anthony

Scott Anthony is the managing partner of Innosight, a co-author with Clay Christensen and solo of *The First Mile* (HBR, 2014). He was shortlisted for the 2015 Thinkers50 Innovation Award.

From Christie Hunter Arscott and Lauren Noël

Dear CEO,

When we asked ICEDR (International Consortium for Executive Development Research) partner companies 'What is your most pressing talent challenge?', they responded: 'Retaining women 5–10 years out of university.' CEOs are still struggling to crack the code on how to attract, retain and advance women, and more specifically, early career/millennial women.

Due to changing demographics, investing in early career talent – both male and female – is critically important for companies around the world. Millennials are projected to account for 75 per cent of the workforce by 2025.

Early career talent – both men and women – face challenges within the first ten years of their careers and struggle to get the support they need to navigate these obstacles. Junior talent highly values targeted and customized development, yet they find that their companies could be more effective at helping them grow their skills. In our ICEDR study of men and women age 22–35, 97 per cent said it was important for their organizations to contribute to developing their skills, yet only 67 per cent found their organizations to be effective at this.

These early career challenges are heightened for women. A Catalyst study shows that women lag men from their very first professional jobs in job placement, compensation and engagement. Additionally, research highlights that (in comparison to their male peers) women's ambition and confidence significantly erode after only two years in their first job.

Companies incur substantial financial costs when they lose early career women. Recently published data highlights that women job hop more than men. Research shows that the cost of losing an employee can be up to 2x their annual salary.

Companies are investing significant funds in an effort to change the gender balance within their organizations and advance women to the upper echelons of management, yet these efforts are still falling short. Even CEOs with the best intentions and the resources to back these intentions are not seeing significant returns on their investments. Women still only represent 2–3 per cent of CEOs in S&P 500 companies. 'Intention' + 'Investment' + 'Effort' are not equating to 'Results'.

To date, most talent strategies have focused on women at the senior leadership, executive or board level but research shows this is too late. To achieve systemic change, companies must focus attention on women at earlier career stages.

McKinsey research shows that if companies could raise the number of women in mid-level management roles who make it to the next level by 25 per cent, it would significantly alter the shape of the pipeline.

CEOs should be asking themselves:

Have our existing efforts to retain and advance women been successful in significantly improving the gender balance in senior leadership positions?

If not, have our efforts to date primarily focused on women at the senior leadership, executive or board level? Do we have any programmes or initiatives specifically targeting early career women?

How can we better equip early career women to navigate the challenges they face within the first ten years of their careers?

So, what is our proposed solution? How would we advise you to proceed?

Target Early Career Women: CEOs have a promising opportunity to capture by focusing on women early on in the pipeline. To date, most talent strategies have targeted women at the senior leadership, executive or board level but research shows this is too late. There is no such thing as too early!

Equalize Access: To truly change the shape of the female talent pipeline, leaders should seek to create inclusive programmes accessible to *all* early career women (not just high potential women). By democratizing access to resources, support, connections and targeted learning, organizations will increase the probability that their efforts will result in significant demographic and number shifts later on in the pipeline.

Ask, Don't Assume: Talk with your people not about your people: Instead of talking about early career women, talk with early career women. Steer clear of developing retention strategies in board rooms full of executives and HR leaders (far removed from the day-to-day existence and input of the women you are trying to retain). Instead, seek to understand the needs, desires and priorities of your people.

Focus on Challenging Transitions: In our research, early career women ranked 1. 'Transition from university to first job', 2. 'Changing of Roles: Transition from first job to a new role' and

3. 'Transition into motherhood and having a family with young children' as the top three challenging transitions they face. These transition points are critical junctures where women are likely to leak out of the pipeline and where leaders can provide essential support, connectivity and resources to plug those holes and retain women as they navigate challenging obstacles.

Address Challenges beyond Family and Flexibility: While options for flexibility and work-life integration are important, the bottom line is that motherhood is not the primary reason why talented women are leaving organizations. Focusing retention strategies on this alone, without also considering other factors important to early career women, will ultimately jeopardize retention and advancement efforts. Leaders should seek to build their talent strategies around what matters most to early

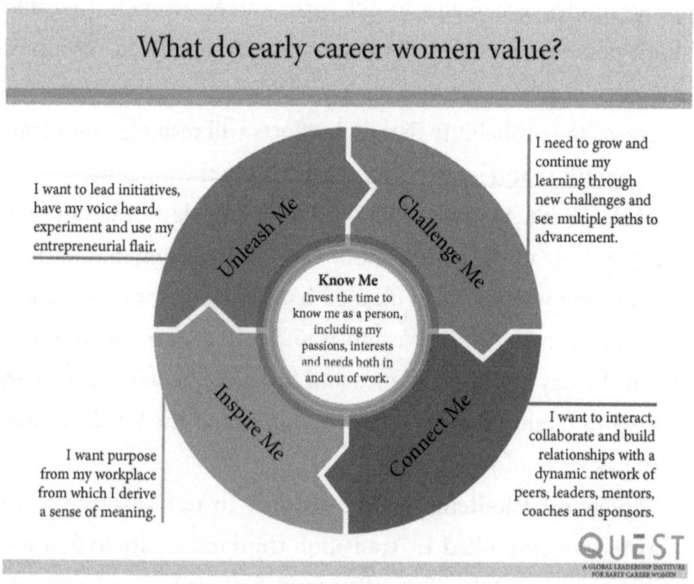

career women, including feeling: understood as an individual, challenged to grow and take on new challenges, connected to a dynamic network, inspired with purpose and unleashed to lead and innovate.

Christie Hunter Arscott and Lauren Noël

Christie Hunter Arscott is Principal of QUEST (www.herquest.org), a global institute for early career women. She was one of the first Rhodes Scholars to pursue a Master's degree in Women's Studies at the University of Oxford, where she researched women and gendered leadership styles.

Lauren Noël is Managing Director of QUEST. Prior to leading QUEST, she worked with the Young Presidents' Organization and at Harvard Business School. She was named an emerging leader by the *Boston Business Journal* and holds an MBA from the MIT Sloan School of Management.

From Marco Bertini

Put the Customers' Money Where Your Mouth Is

Dear CEO,

In all likelihood, your enterprise strives to take good care of its customers. You listen, gathering insights that can help differentiate your solutions from those of competitors in a meaningful way. You also observe. Like never before, you can map the journeys of customers across traditional and virtual touch points, and engineer experiences that engage and spur loyalty. Finally, internally, you probably continue to tweak the organization to relate better to the market: smarter metrics, smarter incentives, customer champions and so on.

All of this is excellent. Yet, from where I stand, it is only half the battle.

In my experience, even the most customer-centric venture reverts to old habits when it is time to turn all of this hard work into cash you can bank. When it comes to the revenue you generate, rather than taking a hard look at customers, many take a hard look at what they sell.

Think about it: No customer wants to buy time, yet this is exactly what professional service firms continue to invoice. No customer wants to buy goods, gadgets, components or instruments for the sake of owning them, yet this is what most brands tag with a price.

In short, I fear that your revenue strategy does not reflect the needs and wants of the market – at least, not to the same extent as the rest of the business. It is instinctive to look within when deciding how to price anything. What did it cost us to bring this offer to market? What is an acceptable return on our investment? Addressing questions of this type is prudent, but it should only be the starting point.

Ask more questions: Do you often miss a sale because customers cannot access (physically or financially) the product or service when the opportunity arises? Do customers routinely run out? Are you forcing customers to purchase something that they seldom use, or that they use only in part? Do you tie your revenue to the outcomes that you promise, or are the two mostly independent?

If the answer is 'yes' to any of the above, then your revenue strategy is probably *wasteful* – it forces customers to take on unnecessary risk. In the past, this was not necessarily a big deal. Customers had little choice but to do as told. Today, thanks to several technologies, it is different. In fact, what I am writing about often fuels the threat of disruption in an industry.

Let me explain. In this era of cloud computing, constant connectivity, the Internet of Things and micro transactions it is increasingly possible for customers to pay for what they want when they want it. We can now record every usage occasion, turn almost any good into a service, break down expenses to fit budgets big and small, coordinate users who tolerate sharing the same asset and measure results cheaply and with precision. Customers struggle to access what you sell? Consider a subscription plan. Customers seldom use your asset, or they only use it in part? Consider a sharing platform. Consider unbundling. Customers take on the risk of product failure or malfunction? Consider a pay-for-performance metric or contract.

The troubling part is that it only takes one visionary to upset the status quo in a market. These opportunities are available to you, and they are probably already in the mind of the next start-up.

In sum, be careful. You have done the hard work to differentiate your offering – to find a 'blue ocean'. Do not throw it away by forcing customers into an exchange that is inefficient to them. I like to think of customers as magnets. They have the money you chase, and they have the final word. It is reasonable to assume that if the opportunity arises, they prefer to do business with a brand that puts their money where its mouth is.

Take steps towards this new reality.

Marco Bertini

Marco Bertini (marcobertini.com) is Associate Professor and Department Head of the marketing subject area at ESADE in Barcelona. He was previously a professor at London Business School. He was included in the Thinkers50 Radar for 2017.

From Julian Birkinshaw and Jonas Ridderstråle

Dear CEO,

We realize you have a lot of things on your plate, so the last thing you need is another new strategic initiative to work on. But please bear with us: the proposal outlined below is actually going to make your life a whole lot easier. Of course, the multitude of issues that your company has to address is going to remain as complex and multifaceted as ever, but if you take our advice you will be able to spread the load a bit more, and get focused more quickly on the important stuff.

You have heard the expression 'teaching an elephant to dance'. In fact, you have probably used a version of it at some point. Like most of your peers, you wish your company was more nimble and responsive, more like some of those Silicon Valley start-ups that get featured in business magazines all the time.

In fact, we would suggest that increasing your 'strategic agility', your capacity to adapt quickly to changes in your business environment, could be the most important and difficult challenge you face right now. We were talking just last week to managers in one of the largest consumer products companies in the world, and they said their biggest barrier to change is their over-engineered formal processes – things like the budgeting process, the performance evaluation system, the stage/gate methodology for reviewing new products. These were high calibre, highly motivated people, all trying their best to make the company a success. And yet the 'system' was holding them back.

Why does everything take such a long time in big companies? We see two linked problems. One is the invisible stranglehold of bureaucracy – everything gets done according to rules and procedures. Of course, the rules aren't always wrong. These management processes were designed by thoughtful, well-intentioned people. But over time they take on a life of their own. They metastasize to address all eventualities, and their linkage to the company's overall goals becomes ever more tenuous.

Many company executives have said they want to move away from bureaucracy towards a 'meritocracy', which puts people and ideas first. This isn't a bad idea. We can all agree that knowledge, or human capital as it is sometimes called, is central to success in today's Information Age. But it turns out that a meritocracy can be just as slow and internally focused as a bureaucracy. We work in the oldest form of meritocracy – the university – and while we hate rules, we love to argue and discuss every issue, and we believe strongly in consensus. Many professional service firms, and indeed quite a lot of traditional business organizations too, have moved in this direction, thanks to this belief that knowledge and learning are the only sustainable sources of competitive advantage. Yet, the sad result is often a form of analysis paralysis where people are highly knowledgeable and can 'talk the talk' but nothing actually gets done.

So what you actually need is not a focus on rules and procedures, nor is it a focus on knowledge and insight – you need a focus on action. We call this model the adhocracy, as distinct from bureaucracy or meritocracy. In practice, it means simplifying your formal processes, reducing the number and size of your cross-functional committees and eliminating some of the centres-of-excellence sitting in headquarters and putting in their place a light-touch, fleet-footed model where small teams are empowered to take action quickly and in direct response to the needs of their users. If you like analogies, think in terms of the special forces units used by the military when operating in enemy territory. It is said that no plan survives contact with the enemy, so adaptability and thinking on your feet is at a premium. In a business context, this means breaking work up into small projects, doing experiments and market tests and adapting quickly to feedback.

We know this change in emphasis will be difficult for many of your managers. When faced with uncertainty, most people default back to what they are comfortable with – typically either a standard operating procedure (bureaucracy) or a review committee (meritocracy). You need to have the courage to push against these instincts. And there are some handy examples you can draw inspiration from in the business world today. For example, the agile movement in software development, and in particular the scrum methodology, is entirely consistent with our notion of adhocracy. Other examples are the beyond budgeting movement and the Holacracy organizing model.

This more action-focused approach to organizing, by the way, requires some pretty big shifts in management style for you and your team. You have to give up some of your traditional sources of power, and you need to start promoting people who challenge the status quo. Ultimately, the adhocracy isn't really an organizing model, it's a state of mind. And if you want to make your company agile and competitive in today's business environment, it should be at the centre of your change agenda.

Julian Birkinshaw and Jonas Ridderstråle

Julian Birkinshaw is Professor of Strategy and Entrepreneurship at London Business School and has written twelve books, including *Becoming a Better Boss*, *Reinventing Management* and *Giant Steps in Management*. He is a Thinkers50 ranked thinker.

Jonas Ridderstråle is the co-author of the international best-sellers *Funky Business* and *Karaoke Capitalism*. He has been included in the Thinkers50 on six occasions. Birkinshaw and Ridderstråle are the authors of *Fast/Forward: Make Your Company Fit for the Future* (Stanford Business Books, 2017).

From Linda Brimm

Dear CEO,

Increased globalization of business has created a reaction in nationalist movements in many countries. Concerns about fairness and a better distribution of the economic gains of globalization have become a worldwide concern. People are raising questions about free-trade agreements and money moving across borders. There are increasing attempts to block some of the benefits of diverse global organizations. It is urgent to figure out how to stay competitive on a global scale. CEOs must address these issues urgently, or they will not be able to compete.

CEOs of global organizations need to identify the potential leaders who have the capacity to work in this ever-changing landscape and lead the changes necessary to build competitive and global organizations that will also be seen as creating greater fairness and opportunity.

An increasing number of talented individuals whom I call 'global cosmopolitans' have lived and benefited from this globalization. While they are the potential leaders for global organizations, global organizations often do not know who they are, do not know how to benefit from their expertise, let alone hire them or retain them.

Global cosmopolitans are this generation's rapidly expanding and talented population of highly educated, multilingual people that have lived, worked and studied for extensive periods in different cultures. They have grown up in a political/economic context and technological reality that has significantly impacted their world view and skill set. This is a population that CEOs must get to know and develop, since they have the potential to be outstanding leaders.

Their backgrounds and life histories make them particularly suited for the new organizational reality. Their deep knowledge of multiple cultures and a global perspective, their experience with complicated dilemmas and change from the lives they lead, contributes to developing the very skills that are necessary to lead in a global economy.

Each cultural experience provides an opportunity to understand the use of multiple lenses and perspectives and to gain respect and build bridges with people from diverse backgrounds. Managing change on multiple levels is normal for them. They have had to reinvent themselves and experiment with new identities and new ways of thinking. Their 'kaleidoscopic vision' provides them with a perspective on change, that the patterns will look different, that some aspects of the new vision might be missing pieces, yet with another turn of the kaleidoscope the some key pieces can return or reappear in a very different pattern.

They understand the impact that the global reach of organizations can have. They have frequently developed a global mindset and the necessary cognitive flexibility to address the complex issues of globalization and the very skills that are necessary to lead in a global economy. While they can understand thinking locally, they have the capacity to think globally. They have experience moving knowledge across borders and then adapting it to a local culture.

Unfortunately, businesses have had difficulty identifying, developing and managing these individuals.

The conflict between the political and business forces around globalization is very charged and requires people who can live and lead in this confusing space. It requires better identification, development and utilization of this talent.

The questions you need to ask are these:

As a CEO, how do I manage the conflicts between a global perspective and national concerns? Do I need to refine my vision of how to stay globally competitive while being responsive to national cultures? How will I define the path and identify the people that will take on this responsibility and can best make it happen?

Are we able to identify the global cosmopolitans already in our organization? Does my organization know how to manage and develop these people so that we can derive the benefits from their unique experience and keep them from leaving?

As the CEO, are you ready to become actively involved? It is not enough to say it is important to identify and develop global cosmopolitans; it is crucial that you get to know your global cosmopolitans. You and your organization need to develop a way to increase awareness of this high potential group, get involved in their reviews and see how to develop their careers.

While these issues are often delegated to HR or human capital groups, CEOs have to become personally involved to drive the necessary changes. More active involvement in HR reviews is necessary, making this a strategic concern for the business. Placing global cosmopolitans on boards as well as in strategic leadership positions will reflect the diversity in the organization and send a crucial signal to people wishing to stay involved in the organization.

Identifying and developing global cosmopolitans requires sensitivity to both individual and cultural differences in order to make this happen. Creative solutions are necessary to identify and develop people of diverse background experience.

Global cosmopolitans are often not that obvious. One of the skills that they can develop is adaptability. This adaptability is often what I refer to as the one edge of a two-edged sword of mobility. Sometimes they adapt so smoothly, and they do not see or know how to take advantage of the other side of the sword, their difference. Without helping people see the potential strengths they have developed on their global journeys, the strengths can feel so natural to the individuals that they often do not know how to articulate them or share them, or they continue to use the one edge without sharing the power of the other one.

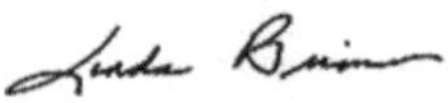

Linda Brimm

Linda Brimm is Emeritus Professor of Organizational Behaviour at INSEAD. Trained as a clinical psychologist, she also works with both individuals and families at a centre she co-founded in Paris. She is the author of *Global Cosmopolitans, The Creative Edge of Difference* (globalcosmopolitans.com).

From David Burkus

Dear CEO,

You have a lot of jobs, a lot of responsibility rests on your shoulders. From overseeing the ongoing cycle of strategic planning to being first to respond to a crisis with just the right words – well scripted but with just the right amount of spontaneity and sincerity – we've come to expect you to be able to do almost anything and respond to almost any demand.

Navigating all of these demands, however, can make it difficult to keep your eye on the north star and identify the focus of the company, to find the 'what we do' that becomes the company's real purpose.

Making this even more difficult are the constant changes and technological advances experienced over the past few decades … or even the past decade. It's likely when you started your career the company looked a lot different from how it looks today. The role of a CEO looked a lot different then from how it looks today. Amid all these changes, it can become difficult to find the way to manage a company – to manage a workforce – that will stand the test of time, that will remain effective no matter that changes.

I recently finished a book, *Under New Management*, that describes what some of the smartest leaders are changing about their leadership in order to manage talent in this new age. And while I found it nearly impossible to reduce the ideas in that book to one maxim, one piece of advice that would always be true – one of the CEOs I interviewed managed to do just that. Here's what he said:

> Great leaders don't innovate the product; they innovate the factory.

Great leaders of great companies don't focus solely on innovating their product or service to provide a sustainable competitive advantage or release a disruptive innovation. Those are important, no doubt. But great leaders know that those only come *after* one has innovated the factory, a metaphor for our organization to allow its people to do their best work.

And this has been true for over 100 years. It was true when Fredrick Taylor innovated the literal factory floor of countless manufacturing companies to produce unheard of productivity. And it's true today for the various CEOs that are rethinking how work gets done to bring out the best in their knowledge workers.

Not sure where to start innovating your factory? Let me offer one small suggestion there:

> Eliminate something.

Specifically, find out what practices or procedures are blocking your people from doing their best work – what rules are causing frustration – and get rid of them or at least one of them. We often think of new management innovations as things to be added, adopted, implemented and the like. But many of the most innovative workplaces got that way because leaders saw what was blocking people from reaching their potential and they eliminated it. When Thierry Breton of Atos found that internal emails were overloading his employees and stealing their focus, he eliminated it and set a course to become a zero email company. When Reed Hastings (the CEO of Netflix) found that their standard vacation policy was causing administrative headaches and triggering feelings of distrust among individuals in the company, he eliminated it and increased the trustworthy behaviour of all employees. When Dane Atkinson (CEO of SumAll) saw that salary secrecy was causing strife and division among employees and keeping them from earning their fair share, he made a commitment to openness and transparency.

It might not be email, vacation policies or salary information that's causing your employees undue stress or blocking them from reaching their full potential. But whatever it is, eliminating it will be the first step to innovating your factory.

David Burkus

David Burkus is a professor at the Oral Roberts University. He is the author of *The Myths of Creativity* (Jossey-Bass, 2013) and *Under New Management* (Houghton Mifflin, 2016). He was included in the Thinkers50 Radar for 2016.

From Tomas Chamorro-Premuzic

Dear CEO,

What is the most pressing challenge or issue facing the world's CEOs today?

I am generally somewhat reluctant to emphasize the 'today' or 'future' elements underlying this type of question. When we focus on the present or future of leadership, we inevitably end up over-hyping complexity and change when in fact the fundamentals of leadership have remained pretty much intact over the past few thousands of years. Sure, the specific context and preoccupation of businesses may change over the course of decades, but 99 per cent of the problems and challenges CEOs face today are identical to the problems most leaders have faced for hundreds of years, namely: (a) can you set the right strategy or direction for your followers or subordinates; (b) can you keep their egos in check so they perform as a cohesive unit that displays collaborative behaviours to create a true synergy; (c) can you provide a sense of purpose and sell a vision to them that explains why what they are doing matters; and (d) can you keep your own derailers in check, behave with integrity and put the welfare of the organization ahead of your own interests? If CEOs got these issues right, they will not need to worry about any novel challenges or the unexpected problems that the future may bring. And if they get them wrong, it is irrelevant how good they are at solving seemingly novel problems.

For most CEOs the big pending challenge is to fix the basic human capital issues that disrupt their organizations. Although twenty years have passed since McKinsey first introduced the idea of a war for talent, which stated that in order to be successful companies must master the art of identifying, developing, engaging and retaining talented employees, the state of affairs for most business is rather bleak. In fact, one could argue that the war *for* talent has become the war *on* talent: 70 per cent of people are not engaged at work; 65 per cent of the workforce can be considered passive job seekers; and a growing number of people ditch traditional employment in favour of self-employment and entrepreneurship, where they will end up working more to earn less and contribute less to the overall economy. Therefore, if CEOs want to be successful they need to fix their talent management issues so that they can attract and retain top talented people: the vital few who are able to make a big difference and help their organizations outperform their competitors. The most successful organizations I know have CEOs who understand the strategic value of HR and work very closely with their HR departments to drive growth and success.

One thing that has changed is expectations: in the developed world most people now expect to have interesting and well-paid jobs, but that is just not possible. These unrealistic expectations backfire: if we all want to date Brad Pitt or Angelina Jolie, most of us will be single for ever. If you think about it, 100 years ago, with the advent of Taylorism and assembly lines, people were just content having a steady job and being productive. Today we are living in the age of the spiritual workaholic and most people want meaning, purpose and a sense of self-actualization. On the other hand, most companies think they are able to attract star employees but the reality is that star employees come in small quantities and they can choose the top businesses in the world – so companies also aim higher than they should. As a result, the employment market is highly inefficient: people complain that their jobs are unrewarding and dull, and companies complain that they can't find key talent for their critical roles. Successful leaders will manage expectations, both in their firms and in prospective employees, in order to build an engaged and productive workforce.

So, what key question or questions should CEOs be asking themselves?

The main question is this: what can I offer to people so that they choose to come and work for me, knowing what to expect and motivated to achieve what I want to achieve with this business? Of course, CEOs should not focus most of their energies in addressing this issue. Instead they must find a competent HR or talent management leader who can implement the right human capital strategy to outperform their competitors.

Traditionally, CEOs have strong training in strategy, finance or operations. The missing part is being good with people: being a shrewd judge of character, knowing how to inspire and manage others and being able to combine intuition with data and facts in order to create a high-performing team. In that sense, top CEOs are just like top sports coaches: think Sir Alex Ferguson rather than Marissa Mayer.

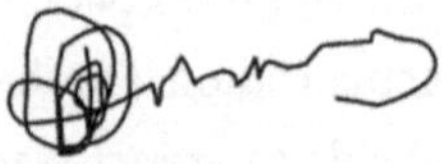

Tomas Chamorro-Premuzic

Tomas Chamorro-Premuzic (www.drtomascp.com) is a University College London and Columbia academic as well as CEO of the assessment company, Hogan Assessments. Chamorro-Premuzic is author of a number of books including *Confidence* (Profile, 2013). He was shortlisted for the 2015 Thinkers50 Talent Award.

From Henry Chesbrough

Dear CEO,

One of your top responsibilities as CEO of the organization is to ensure its future. In particular, the organization needs to grow, to provide more opportunities for its staff, more value for its customers and more returns for its owners. Growth must be at the top of your agenda.

Yes, innovation can be expensive, and too often organizations treat it as a luxury good: much desired in good times, but something to be postponed or reduced in bad times. Given the weak recovery from the financial crisis and the prevailing political uncertainty, this is the state of play in many industries. Too many CEOs give only lip service to innovation.

An alternative approach is better: imagine your organization without having to spend on innovation. At first, everything is great; in fact, there are more profits because of the savings from eliminating spending on innovation. But soon your products and services start to atrophy. Competitors who continued to innovate start to win key accounts and market share from you. Your prices come under increasing pressure, as you fight to hold on. Margins start to decline. Customers become frustrated with the lack of needed improvements. If you extend this scenario farther, you could find yourself out of business before too long.

So innovation is not a luxury, it is a necessity. Managed well, it can deliver more topline revenue, sustain stronger margins and improve market share and customer satisfaction.

In sum, here are some critical questions for you to ask, to get more growth out of your investments in innovation:

- What knowledge already exists in this area? Who are the leaders?
- Who outside our organization thinks our approach is a good idea? Who is willing to collaborate with us and share the costs and risks?
- What percentage of the patents that we own do we actually use? What do we do now with the patents we don't use?
- What are we doing to experiment with new business models in our organization? What are we doing to scale them?

The solution is to open up your innovation process. Bringing in ideas and technologies from outside will help you address more opportunities. It will help you move faster, since you can build on what has already been developed versus having to start from scratch. It will reduce cost, since you only need to pay for what you use, leaving to others the value from other uses. It will also manage risk, since your collaborators bear part of the costs in the projects. It even supplies some validation, as you see whether external parties are as interested in the projects as you are. It's the same logic for why venture capital investors syndicate their investments: you get more eyes looking at the opportunity, and you get to deploy more capital for those opportunities. As a result, you get 'more shots on goal' from greater openness, because the same resources can support more initiatives.

Managing innovation well also means allowing unused ideas and technologies to go outside your organization. Too often, potentially valuable ideas and technologies sit on the shelf inside your company and have nowhere to go to test their value outside. (Think of all the patents you own, and ask yourself how many of those patents are actually used in your business!). A promising engineer might have to meet with twenty or more investors, in order to find the money to try her idea. But if one investor says yes, she gets to try. Inside your organization, that same promising engineer might also have to talk to twenty or more people to find money for their idea. If any one of those twenty says no, though, she is effectively blocked.

Which process is going to support more innovation?

Letting your unused ideas go outside provides you another benefit: free-market research on alternative business models. Once the idea leaves your building, other parties will look at it with different perspectives. They may envisage a very different business model to exploit the idea from the business model of your organization. It is quite likely that a new initiative will 'pivot' multiple times in the course of pursuing its future, as the project seeks to find early customers willing to buy and defines what it is that these customers will buy. All of this happens with Other People's Money, not yours. If the venture finds a good fit with the market, you have an option: take a piece of the growth, or reacquire the venture and scale it inside, or do nothing. And you now know about another way to create and capture value for all the many activities going on inside your organization.

Instead of the laboratory being the world you depend upon for your future, make the world your laboratory for ensuring your future instead.

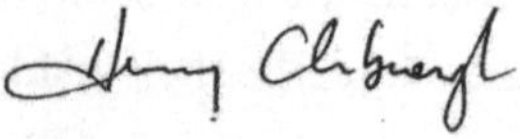

Henry Chesbrough

Henry Chesbrough is Faculty Director of the Garwood Center for Corporate Innovation at the UC Berkeley-Haas School of Business. He originated and developed the concept of Open Innovation. He is a Thinkers50 ranked thinker.

From Sangeet Paul Choudary

Dear CIO,

I value your time and will get straight to the point: To succeed in the digital age, you need to re-evaluate your business architecture.

Like many of your peers, you believe in the importance of digital transformation. However, most digital transformation initiatives merely focus on changes in enterprise infrastructure and market engagement. To be effective, digital transformation needs to focus on a rearchitecture of the firm's core business model itself.

Technology is rapidly changing how firms create value and compete. Across industries, there is a concerted shift away from resource utilization and process efficiency towards user-centric value creation.

In our traditional view of technology in the enterprise, we saw technology as an essential infrastructure that brings efficiency to our existing resource-centric business models. Over the last two decades, IT has been used to drive greater process efficiency in our existing systems.

In a world of connectivity and data, technology is no longer merely a vehicle for higher efficiency. The opportunity of digital transformation is not in making our resource-centric business models more efficient through the employment of digital technologies.

The real opportunity of digital transformation is in building better understanding of markets and restructuring the business model to best serve the ecosystem of partners and consumers that engage with the firm.

Users have greater choice in a connected world and are increasingly distracted. Brands will need to move beyond creating a compelling user experience only. *The businesses most successful at driving profitability from connected users will be the ones that restructure their entire business model around core user behaviours.*

Every user-centric business has a core user behaviour that drives the value created for the user. We understand this when we look at companies like Facebook. Interaction with the news feed is the core user behaviour that drives Facebook's business model. The data and value created through the core user behaviour drive greater profitability. Higher profitability, in turn, reinforces the focus of the business on managing the core user behaviour. This virtuous cycle drives the business model of the most successful user-centric companies. *A firm's successful digital transformation will involve the restructuring of its business model from a resource-driven business model to a more user-centric business model.*

The shift from a resource-centric business model to a user-centric business model is non-trivial. To effectively navigate this shift, you need to manage three key issues that determine successful transformation.

First, the shift to user-centric business models needs to be a strategic priority. It needs to be driven by you as the chief executive. Many organizations are currently leading digital transformation initiatives as a CMO-led or CIO-led initiative.

Many CMO-led transformation initiatives tend to be outside-in and focus on greater user engagement without business model rearchitecture. A lot of CIO-led transformation is more inside-out and focuses on integration of the infrastructure to drive process efficiencies. Neither approach impacts strategy directly. To transform your organization for the digital age, you need to ensure that digital transformation is a strategic priority that you drive so as to merge the outside-in and the inside-out approaches to organizational transformation. It needs to leverage both higher consumer engagement and a digitally integrated infrastructure towards a user-centric business model.

Second, CEOs will need to move their metrics from the measurement of key asset utilization to the measurement of core user behaviours. A user-centric business model ties profitability to the management of core user behaviours. Netflix's profitability is closely aligned with the growing usage of its recommendation system just as Facebook's profitability is directly determined by engagement on the news feed. Effective digital transformation requires execution towards reinforcing these core user behaviours. The choice of user-focused metrics will enable your organization to align itself towards such execution.

Finally, your firm's governance model needs to shift focus from the enterprise to the ecosystem. Traditional governance models focus entirely on internal enterprise governance. As you embrace openness and external participation, you will have to extend governance to external interactions between partners and users.

I believe business model rearchitecture for the digital age will be the single greatest determiner of success. Rearchitect your business model around core user behaviours and design your metrics and governance mechanisms accordingly.

I wish you the very best as you pull apart your business model and restructure it to leverage the power of this connected and data-rich world.

Best regards,

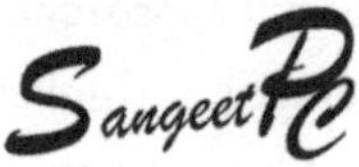

Sangeet Paul Choudary

Sangeet Paul Choudary is the founder and CEO of Platform Thinking Labs (platformed.info). He is co-chair of the MIT Platform Strategy Group, an entrepreneur-in-residence at INSEAD, a global fellow at the Centre for Global Enterprise and an advisor at 500Startups. He is the co-author of *Platform Revolution* and was included in the Thinkers50 Radar list for 2016.

From Enrique Dans

Dear CIO,

In the space of a few years, computers and computing in general has changed dramatically, a change not yet understood by most people in business. Changing the way we understand technology and being able to understand what technology can do for our businesses is a more pressing need with each day that passes. For many years, we saw computers simply as another form of automation. We increasingly use them to carry out any repetitive, tedious or demanding tasks. This is how computers entered corporate environments, taking over routine activities such as calculation, payroll, accounting, etc., as well as those areas where there was a legal requirement for safeguarding information.

Computers were machines that could do the same things as people, but faster, cheaper and with fewer errors. This idea of computing as automation has been a constant in our approach to investing in technology since businesses first started using computers. Some time ago this approach began to change radically. When we see on the news that a computer has beaten Garry Kasparov at chess, won Jeopardy with scores way above those of previous contestants or has annihilated the best Go players in the world, it's clear that we're not talking about the same computing we have known to date: to perform these kinds of feats more is needed than a faster, bigger computer.

The new frontier is now machine learning, and it will bring about a bigger change to the world than the Internet has. This is the kind of change that will decide which companies survive and which disappear. It will change what we mean by work, transforming our societies and all within the next five years.

This means that right now, if a company wants to have any kind of competitive advantage it's going to have to get hold of the data needed to feed machine learning algorithms that are better, more efficient and more competitive than its competitors. It's as simple as that.

For a computer to beat Lee Sedol or Fan Hui, the two best Go players in the world, it has to do more than calculate very quickly. To achieve this, Google not only had to get its hands on the moves made in every game of Go on record and make sure that its machine, AlphaGo, was infinitely better at remembering what it learned, it also had to apply and combine techniques of deep learning and reinforcement learning: pitting the machine against itself, inventing moves that had not been played by a human player, as well as deriving new moves from these, which were later fed back into the system. And so on and so on. The chance of a human making some of the moves played by AlphaGo, which have been praised for their elegance and beauty, has been calculated as one in ten thousand and described as so complex that no human could understand, let alone anticipate them. This is the same process that occurs when every self-driving vehicle on the road automatically contributes to the learning experience of all the self-driving vehicles circulating in the world owned by a particular company. How they are defined and parameterized radically changes the competitive advantages.

That said, the mindset required is not necessarily about winning, but instead improving levels of cooperation between humans and machines and using this to try to solve the many pressing problems we face.

Soon we will have autonomous artificial intelligence. These technologies will be able to take business decisions by studying everything that is going on around them. They will be able to do so in a much more comprehensive, thorough and rigorous way than any team of executives. Others will set the European Central Bank's interest rates, decide tax levels and calculate pension increases. We are entering the most radical change we have experienced in the history of mankind.

Catching this wave is absolutely crucial to our survival: it's the ultimate game changer. Understanding the changes that have taken place in computing as soon as possible and preparing for the bigger change that is coming are absolutely crucial for our company and undoubtedly the most important decision of your life as a director.

Thanking you for your time and attention.

Yours sincerely,

Enrique Dans

Enrique Dans is Professor of Innovation at IE Business School and a prolific blogger at enriquedans.com. Dans is one of the Spanish-speaking world's leading technology opinion formers. He was shortlisted for the 2015 Thinkers50 Digital Award.

From Richard D'Aveni

Navigating Unchartered Waters

Dear CEO,

You're probably hearing a lot about convergence these days:

- Digital-physical – from driverless cars to the Internet of Things to 3D printing, merging products with Internet services.
- Industrial – companies getting hit by rivals out of nowhere as borders between products or geographies go away.
- Functional – thanks to instant communication and 3D printing of prototypes, product development teams are working so closely with manufacturing and marketing that they might as well merge.

Still, convergence tends to be like the weather: everybody talks about it but nobody knows what to do about it. Our conventional strategies assume stable industries and economics. We're stuck in old mindsets while business is being transformed. We've imagined our companies as portfolios of businesses working within defined boundaries. It's time for new metaphors, and my favourite is a school of fish swimming in an ocean without borders that separate the waters.

In this metaphor, each fish is an autonomous being that congregates in schools to improve their chances of finding food and fending off predators. The fish constantly watches their fellows to know what to do, based on a few simple rules such as follow the majority or move towards the successful (fatter) fish. The scouting fish on the edges are looking for threats and opportunities, and they'll often veer off in response. At times the school needs to scatter apart, but the school soon reforms when the danger passes. A migrating school gradually shifts direction as the scouts discover new leads and attract others to follow in their boundary-less world.

Think of any sizeable company as a school, with each fish representing a line of business (LOB). Because of convergence, each LOB is free to swim in many directions. But if they cooperate and loosely influence each other, they generate collective motion that enables most of them to survive and prosper. Their flexibility and autonomy generates a kind of swarm intelligence that better responds to collapsing boundaries between physical and digital goods, industries and even functions.

Here's what the school of fish metaphor means in business terms:

- Coping with a Borderless Competitive Space: Rather than LOBs operating in a collection of distinct markets, a school of LOBs explores the open space for better profit pools. This contrasts with traditional business methods of exploring new markets, where an individual LOB is charged with the task. The entire school collectively self-organizes to explore the ocean, but nevertheless balances the risks and opportunities of changing path. A few fish wander away from the school, moving only a short distance.

Nearby fish follow if they discover something good. This ripples throughout the school, causing the overall school to change direction towards richer ecosystems.

- Free-Flowing Organizations: Each LOB is free to move around the school to be closer to the other LOBs that can help the most, as well as to the outside opportunities. But just as fish on the periphery of the school are easy for sharks to pick off, LOBs will want to stay in synch with the school as a whole. LOBs stay together and avoid collisions not because of strict directions from headquarters, but because of a strict set of cultural norms or simple rules that govern each fish's movements. The better the rules, the better your organization will be able to diverge from what all the other schools are doing and pursue more profitable opportunities.
- Migration Strategies: The school's biggest challenge is deciding where to move. It can't stay in one position for long, because it will exhaust the feeding ground or attract predators, but it's hard to sense where to go. Organizations likewise need to hire more visionaries with good instincts on where opportunities or threats are likely to emerge. They need more Leonardo da Vinci's and fewer analysts. Da Vinci could create the Mona Lisa one day and a robot the next; you will need that kind of free thinking to survive in open, continually shifting markets. Combine that with daring scouts who can tackle promising areas quickly. Blue oceans can't be found by analytics; they have to be discovered.
- Rethink Leadership: The time you were spending on controlling operations can now be used to better explore possibilities. Send out more scouts to check out potential

opportunities or threats. Cast a wide field of investigation, in three dimensions, instead of the usual strategic analysis. Visionaries will be at a premium in a convergent world.

How far you take this advice will depend on how far along you see convergence happening in your industry. But don't assume you'll have much time to move once you see the shifts. In just about every kind of business, digitization is having a strong effect, and it's going to intensify as computers get increasingly powerful.

Convergence is turning every business into a school of fish, wandering in a vast sea of possibilities with predators at every turn.

Sincerely,

Richard D'Aveni

Richard D'Aveni (www.radstrat.com) is Bakala Professor of Strategy at the Tuck School of Business at Dartmouth College. He reinvented the language of strategy with the best-seller *Hypercompetition*. His other books include *Strategic Supremacy*, *Beating the Commodity Trap* and *Strategic Capitalism*. Most recently, in a series of influential articles, D'Aveni has charted the rise of 3D printing and its likely impact on the world of manufacturing. He is a Thinkers50 ranked thinker.

From Niraj Dawar

Markets or Shareholders?

Dear CEO,

There is a fine line between professing free-market capitalism and the subversion of those markets that is crossed in businesses every day.

On the one hand, the ideal of free markets implies open competition in markets where information flows freely, where no single player is powerful enough to influence aggregate demand or supply and where any advantage a company gains is eventually replicated by competitors. On the other, there is the reality of imperfect markets where competition is actively subverted by businesses.

We like to believe in the ideal of free markets because competition, we are convinced, is good for the economy. Competition forces sellers to keep the interests of the buyers at the heart of what they do; competition marginalizes and eliminates inefficient players; and competition for customers and resources spurs innovation, forcing businesses to find better, more efficient ways of doing things. In short, these ideal markets are supposed to lead to an efficient allocation of the economy's resources, making us all better off in the long term.

If there is one principle that business leaders profess to believe in, it is the belief in the efficiency and inherent goodness of free markets.

But in practice, businesses are run by another equally explicit principle, and that is the belief that the goal of a business organization is the maximization of shareholder value. According to this principle, business organizations exist to provide their shareholders with the maximum long-term return on their investment.

This is a worthy goal and a valuable principle because in conjunction with a free market it offers the carrot that ensures the efficient allocation of resources. Businesses that aim to maximize shareholder value in competitive markets will use the economy's resources efficiently.

In a real economy – one that is not your textbook picture-perfect market – the maximization of shareholder value is most efficiently achieved by exploiting market imperfections. Market imperfections are any wrinkles in the market that give one company an advantage over others. And exploiting these, too, is a good thing: the fact that so many businesses have exploited the wrinkle of lower manufacturing costs in China has raised living standards in both China and among its trading partners, and increased shareholder value. Over time, as the wrinkle is exploited, it gets ironed out, and businesses must find other wrinkles.

But it is when companies get into the business of creating and maintaining regulatory wrinkles so that they can continue to exploit them that we run into trouble. Firms that push for government protection in the form of trade barriers, longer patent life or more global application of patents are attempting to keep competitors out. This type of lobbying for protection and favourable regulation undermines markets in many industries in many countries, including telecoms, banking, airlines, energy, infrastructure, pharmaceuticals, etc. Sometimes, this gives rise to comical contradictions: pharmaceutical firms arguing for a lowering of import restrictions in foreign markets but a raising of patent protections, in the same breath.

The result is that we end up with oligopolies – a small number of companies that realize that it is not in their interest to compete too fiercely on price or, indeed, on any other dimension.

In other words, at the same time as we profess a reverence for the markets, we're practicing the subversion of free markets. In a toss-up between advocating more competition for the telecoms sector versus protecting the oligopoly, between shortening the life of pharmaceutical patents and enforcing them globally, we repeatedly find ourselves on the side of the oligopoly. Far from cheering creative destruction, we end up advocating creative obstruction.

The result is a loss of the putative gains of a free market. Sellers have little reason to keep the interest of buyers in mind – they're too busy protecting their sources of advantage (think of telecoms companies); inefficient players are not marginalized or eliminated (think of General Motors); and innovation is not promoted (when was the last time you saw an airline do something innovative rather than cost-cutting?).

Restoring society's eroding faith in capitalism is not something that will happen overnight. Alleviating popular scepticism of businesses may take even longer. But a good place for businesses to start is with some soul searching about where their allegiance resides: with efficient markets in the service of society, or with the creation and promotion of market inefficiencies in the service of oligopolies?

Niraj Dawar

Niraj Dawar is a professor at the Ivey Business School, Western University, Canada. He is the author of *Tilt: Shifting Your Strategy from Products to Customers* (HBR, 2013). He was shortlisted for the 2015 Thinkers50 Strategy Award.

From Erica Dhawan

Dear CIO,

We've got a problem. Old-world business models are forsaking new-world potential. People continue working in silos, while businesses continue supporting workplace cultures that follow such outdated paradigms. Radically new ways of connecting are possible, yet corporations have yet to fully embrace the potential of our hyper-connected age.

Consider this: In the minute it takes to read these 580 words, Twitter users have sent nearly 350,000 tweets, Instagram users have liked 1.73 million posts and Facebook users have sent 3.25 million messages. Behind each of these digital events is a single person, business or organization that is reaching audiences with an immediacy and intimacy never before possible in history. That's hyper-connectivity. I'm talking about channeling this same potential into everyday workplace connections. Are there twenty people on your marketing staff? By empowering them with the tools and strategies to collaborate outside of previous boundaries, you'll exponentially increase the expertise that goes into any solution. You'll allow them to transform what is possible by opening themselves up to new people, ideas and resources – all this without increasing staffing costs. It's possible and the benefits are enormous.

But nothing will happen without change. And without change, business can stagnate. What's needed is to create cultures that incentivize collaboration and help employees reach across silos to access new ideas and expertise, processes to help them work together better and to work better together.

It's an approach that's behind an ambitious project being carried out by Case Western Reserve University, which is currently building a facility the size of 8.5 football fields on the campus of the Cleveland Clinic. When the facility is ready in 2019, it will house Case Western's medical, nursing, dental schools. The goal of educating these groups under the same (very large) roof is to improve collaboration skills. Recognizing that teams are essential to health care in the twenty-first century, Case Western already hosts regular brainstorming sessions in which students from each school debate a diagnosis and treatment plan for fictional patients: 'The root of many of our errors had to do with the fact that our professions were not working effectively together for patient care', said Case Western's vice dean of education, Dr Patricia Thomas.

How do you design a culture of connectional intelligence? I propose a three-step solution:

When facing a problem, think about who else cares. Look beyond your regular circle. Case Western recognized that each of the health care professions were seriously invested in patients' well-being – but their expertise needed to be consolidated. 'Health care is no longer a gladiatorial sport, where you [have] the one health care provider – you know, *mano a mano*, one on one – battling a disease', Dr James Young, a cardiologist who heads the Cleveland Clinic Lerner College of Medicine, told NPR.

Engage the help of this cohort. Think about designing initiatives to inspire this community. Like the student debates about patient care plans, bringing together disparate groups with a shared goal will help everyone get used to the idea of collaboration. And show them just how much is to be learned from the expertise of others.

Design a way to sustain this community. For Case Western, it was a $500 million facility. You can do it often within the bounds of your own company.

Erica Dhawan

Erica Dhawan (ericadhawan.com) is the CEO of Cotential, a consulting firm that helps organizations maximize collaboration across teams, business units and customers. She is also the co-author of the best-seller *Get Big Things Done: The Power of Connectional Intelligence* (St Martin's Press, 2015). She was selected on the Thinkers50 Radar for 2016.

From Mark Esposito

Dear CEO,

The most pressing issue I see today is the failure of politics in several democracies, unable to drive our growth towards an integrative model of inclusion, tolerance and prosperity. At the same time, the persistent low growth in our economies pushes organizations even more towards the side effects of volatility, with emotional markets that feel a sense of loss on how we can restart our economic engines and build new inroads for the kind of economic infrastructure we need, in order for us to navigate safely among the new tenets of the century.

The ongoing fluctuations of markets and the inescapable accelerations of emerging economies are sending distress signals to our societies, which are plagued by political impasses and lack of governability, hence making the role of business leaders particularly challenging. At the same time, our analytical tools have become more complex but the predictive assumption of events has not necessarily changed from the undercurrents of the previous industrial models. The intersection between linear reality and incremental valuation, with the increasingly complex socio-economic condition of the world, makes it hard for business to make decisions and the previous algorithm expensively ineffective.

The way we assess risk today has not necessarily changed from the way we did it in the past. We continue to rely on data which is primarily captured at the macro level and which does not model the experience of reality any more. There is sense of inadequacy between the way we collect data and the way data is misrepresentative of the real state of play of the world.

Our models of control of variables (consumers, markets, pricing, etc…) continues to think of business as analytical as it can be, with a myriad of frameworks and protocols and processes that have de-humanized business.

Society these days, though, is no longer following trajectories that echo the past.

Every organization, client or start-up shapes our socio-economic landscape with a unique and novel business proposition/model, which generates the richest epoch in history in terms of opportunities and ideas. Large macro trends are shaping new plots for our societies, which will inexorably transform it, and our ability to navigate and make sense of those trends will be the new competitive analysis of firms. This requires urgent action because major events are developing in the *chemistry* of our socio-economic structure (economic geography, demographic evolution, resource scarcity and rising inequality) but our current modus operandi is still anchored on anachronistic views of the world.

The key question I invite you to consider when you are talking to yourself about the direction of the world but also the direction of your own organization as well as your personal life is how can we integrate asymmetry, lack of order and increasing complexity in our own default thinking and drive decisions and scenarios by embracing the monumental changes that the last thirty years have brought to our societies. How can you integrate a new rationale of 'sense-ability' in which business becomes much more humanized, closer to the buzz of society and a catalyst for positive change? How can you thrive and succeed in a world in which knowledge is no longer the differentiating factor and the capital is no longer the primary requirements of success? How can you frugally innovate and improve the state of the world, by providing accessible innovations and solutions to the varied tiers of our global society? How can you converge, unify, intermediate, bind, integrate and include diversity as part of our intangible assets and build from it?

While the above questions may look daunting and overwhelming, they are just puncture points of a greater unleashing of potential that your organizations can lead as proponents of the future. So in the spirit of collaboration, I invite you to the following tasks:

- Build circular economies in your value chains, so you can decouple growth from resources. This will make you a fair player and will allow you to save costs.
- Build your *raison d'etre* on people and put them always at the centre of what defines your choices in life. Don't objectivize reality. There isn't such a thing!
- Use your capital and your financial acumen to finance those tasks and projects that have the potential to innovate our world by creating new jobs.
- Don't measure business in a strict financial manner only. Find complimentary ways to integrate nonfinancial measurements into your key decisions.

- Use artificial intelligence and automation to enhance people's lives, not to replace them or increase the financial performance solely.
- Challenge the status quo of your organization if you feel that the ghosts of past choices are handcuffing your decisions today.
- Be humble and the world will open to you. Be a steward and the world will serve you. Be kind with those in need so they will become your most loyal allies. Do not fear the future, be it.

My conclusive wish is to see you as one of the architects who will shape our society and business through the challenges ahead of us. As a son, a husband and a father, I need your help to give our future generation a chance to reach and breach new important frontiers.

Thank you
Warmly,

Mark Esposito

Mark Esposito teaches at the Harvard Extension School and is a tenured professor at Grenoble Graduate School of Business and a senior associate at the University of Cambridge Institute in Sustainability Leadership. He is also an adjunct professor at IE Business School in Spain.

Esposito is the author and co-author of nine books, including *From Hubris to Disgrace* (Routledge, 2015) and *Understanding How the Future Unfolds* (with Terence Tse, Lioncrest Publishing, 2017). He was among the up-and-coming thinkers on the Thinkers50 Radar in 2016.

From Alessandro di Fiore

Dear CEO,

What you really need to know and understand is that, contrary to what you may read, analytics get you only so far. Leading organizations also require that most elusive and human of qualities: judgement. The capability to generate and apply insights and qualitative judgements to innovation is a key competitive advantage or, at least, should be.

The trouble is that most companies use a number-driven approach to innovation. Companies invest heavily in developing analytical skills. In recent years, investments have poured into analytics and big data to increase organizational analytical power. Innovation processes have been re-engineered, or over-engineered, with stage-gate processes equipped with financial evaluation tools to support the go/no go decisions and the release of resources at each stage. In their search for numbers, analysts look for benchmarks, from which they can extrapolate impressive-looking business cases and forecasts. Before you know it, the decision has been taken and the company committed to a me-too innovation.

The result is that qualitative perceptions don't get an airing. Strategy and innovation should not be a mere exercise of analytical power, but a qualitative process in which the analysis serves insights born out of individual observation and reflection, rather than the other way around.

Why do business leaders struggle so much in incorporating qualitative judgement into their innovation decisions? Our research and consulting experience uncovered two main causes.

First is what can be called Schumpeter's bias. We all pay lip service to Schumpeter's vision of the lone and creative entrepreneur. This image is so entrenched that people unconsciously tend to believe that the magic of an insight is not replicable. Many business leaders believe that we depend on 'individual' genetic talent. But scientific evidence of the last thirty years proves just the opposite.

A famous study on identical twins aged between fifteen and twenty-two years found that while 80 per cent of IQ differences were attributable to genetics, only around 30 per cent of the performance on creativity tests could be explained that way. Many of the traits we assume to be genetically determined are in fact the product of one's environment. That's a tremendously significant finding in support of the idea that we can work on learning and improving our creativity.

Of course, not every child will be a Leonardo da Vinci, nor will every young manager be a Steve Jobs. But people who point to that fact are missing the one really important truth about creativity: there's Creativity as in genius (the big C) and creativity as in attitude, thinking ability and mindset (the little c). We tend to muddle these two quite different types of creativity.

For example, if you dig into the backstory of Apple, you'll soon realize that it wasn't all about Steve Jobs. He, actually, was wrong a lot of the times. If it had been entirely up to him, Apple would have never opened the App Store. What made Apple great was the combination of Jobs' genius with the little c of the people he worked with and who weren't afraid to express their own ideas. Jobs thought that as well – not, perhaps, in his first spell at the company, but certainly in his second. When asked what he thought was his most important creation, Jobs, rather than mentioning the iPod or iPhone, said it was Apple, the company. He claimed that 'making an enduring company was both harder and more important than making a great product'.

Arguably, little c creativity is more critical in business than the big C.

The second element at work is discomfort with qualitative judgements. Measuring is comforting. Companies, mostly large ones, need to maintain some kind of control over processes and playing the management-by-numbers-game makes decision makers feel more confident. Moreover, the act of measurement is generally seen as a guarantee of unbiased results. Enraptured by the Holy Grail of quantitative analysis, business leaders are so obsessed by numbers that they rarely question their guidance. Preoccupied with issues such as predictability and control, they have become increasingly suspicious of qualitative perceptions.

However comforting it might be to stick with what you can measure, leadership isn't about feeling comfortable. It's about catching opportunities as they occur, even when the numbers suggest otherwise.

Consider the story of Nespresso by Nestlè, which has become Europe's leading brand of premium-portioned coffee. Nespresso machines brew espresso from coffee aluminium, a type of pre-apportioned single-use container of various high-quality coffees and flavourings. The Nespresso brand took off when it stopped targeting offices and started marketing itself to households. Behavioural evidence on how households would respond to the new concept was poor and suggested that consumers' intentions to purchase did not meet quantitative threshold requirements set by market research protocol at Nestlè. Jean-Paul Gaillard, a young marketing head of Nespresso at the time, believed strongly in this idea and, thanks to his skilful interpretation of the data, convinced the company to take the risk. If he had only listened to quantitative research, the concept would have never got off the ground.

Analysis is useful. No question. But, the reality is that judgement is the driving power behind innovation. Good luck.

Yours sincerely,

Alessandro di Fiore

Alessandro di Fiore (adifiore@ecsi-consulting.com) is the founder and CEO of the European Centre for Strategic Innovation (www.ecsi-consulting.com). and ECSI Consulting. He was listed on the Thinkers50 Radar 2016.

From Peter Fisk

The 10x Leader

Dear CEO,

You're busy. You're focused. On today. On delivery. On results.

That's good, but not enough. It's natural to have your head down, managing. It's not easy to have your head up, leading.

Relentless change, disruptive technology, millennial consumers are keywords of our time. So ubiquitous that we ignore them. But they matter. The next ten years will see more change than the last 250 years. By 2025, human brains will be simulated for $1,000, 8 billion consumers will be hyper-connected and Elon Musk will take us to Mars.

Markets have changed, customers have changed (and will change even faster). How has your business changed? How have you?

Whilst the world has never been more accessible – so many people with so much discretionary spend, an infinite choice of business and brands, enabled by automation and intelligence – significant growth is elusive. Finding new ideas is not easy. Making them happen is much harder. Uncertainty saps confidence, talent fights structure, customers distrust brands and today overrules tomorrow.

You are the leader of innovation and growth

Why is it so hard? Because most companies exist in a 10 per cent world. Business plans that deliver 10 per cent more than last year are good enough. Most innovation still focuses on products, and so usually becomes derivative, 10 per cent better. This is incrementalism. Or in an accelerating world, it's called standing still. Yet customers have higher aspirations and expectations than ever, conditioned by their experiences with other companies, often in other sectors. Same for investors.

Think about today's fast growth businesses, like taxi to food delivery platform Uber ($68 bn in seven years), China's electronics giant Xiaomi ($46 bn in six years), car-sharing firm Didi Chuxing ($34 bn in four years) and peer-to-peer accommodation with Airbnb ($30 bn). Most recently, add examples like millennial news channel Vice Media ($4 bn), online educator Udacity ($2 bn) and local delivery bikers Deliveroo ($1 bn). Way back in history, ten years ago, none of them existed.

Yet we feel more confident in trying to stretch our old models of success, rather than creating new ones. We hope that the formula that made us great will continue to serve us well. We try to extrapolate past market success into a discontinuous future. Einstein called it insanity (trying to solve a new problem with the same old thinking). We need to deliver today, to sustain cash and confidence, but we also need to create tomorrow.

Think 10x rather than 10 per cent

Progress happens when we think bigger. When we see a bigger picture, we stretch our ambition, reframe our context and get inspired by new opportunities. This is not about technology itself, but about solving bigger problems and moving the world forwards. In an ideas economy it is not how big you are, but how you think that matters.

Thinking ten times better is not that hard. Start from the future back, and you quickly redefine your market, not just your business. How can you create the future on your terms? Set yourself a bigger challenge, and you inspire new ways to solve a problem. How can we make a car that travels at 500 mpg not just 50 mpg? Or most simply, think like a customer, and you see new insights and opportunities. How can we help you grow, or live better?

10x thinking doesn't actually require ten times the effort or time. Maybe two or three times. By spending a bit longer thinking you see opportunities not before considered, you create more ideas and see new connections, shape stronger and more distinctive solutions and build energy and collaboration in your teams.

'Yes but, …' I hear you say. You need to deliver today as well. Every company needs a blend of 10x and 10 per cent thinking. The thing is, by thinking bigger about your future, you will redefine your short-term priorities too. You have more purpose and direction. Your people feel more ambitious and energized. Your customers and investors too. Leaders amplify the potential of others.

Ideas, of course, are not enough. You need to make them happen. In markets that have changed. Where customers trust their friends more than any brand, and increasingly seek more personal, collaborative solutions, often free. And where value chains are ecosystems, distribution channels are non-linear networks and every business has to be digital and physical.

10x thinking delivers exponential growth

So how do you convert this bigger thinking into 10x impact, or in other words, into profitable, sustainable, exponential growth? Exponential thinking is non-linear, it is about harnessing the power of multiplication, or for business, the power of ideas that spread further and faster and with more impact and value. As CEO your job is to amplify the potential of your team, and thereby also to amplify the potential of your business.

There are three pillars to exponential growth:

- **Addictive ideas**. People are inspired by ideas that do more for them, open up new possibilities, enable them to achieve more. They seek ideas with purpose and passion. They look for resonance like sports fans with FanDuel and spread them contagiously like Snap. Such ideas emerge out of deeper insights, turned quickly into prototypes to test, inspired by richer collaborations and learning from parallel markets with similar experiences. These ideas are spread by smarter design, liquid storytelling and shared participation.

- **Innovation accelerators.** Ideas happen faster with an entrepreneurial mindset – one that thrives on experiments (launch early and learn fast, like GE's FastWorks), recognizing that much can be done by partners better and cheaper, dematerializing ideas so that they are created in ecosystems (like ARM, the semiconductor business that out-thinks Intel) and then focusing innovation on business models (unusual channels to market, adding new revenue streams, whilst removing risk and cost).
- **Market multipliers.** Launch day is day 1. Markets are networks, so make the networks work – harnessing the collective B2B impact of distribution partners and the C2C power of social media. Contagious ideas spread fast when connections and advocacy are facilitated and become valuable. Work with the people customers trust. Michelle Phan (the world's top YouTuber), for example, is the most trusted voice in beauty. Build communities of people who share a passion and become your best marketplaces. Realize the benefits of collective ownership, participation and achievement.

Of course, the effects are most obvious and easily implemented in small companies (in fact, why do you need to be big when the most important asset is the idea, focused on the most profitable niches)? Think of WhatsApp for example. The free messaging service rising to $19bn of value over three years with only seventeen employees. In just a short time, its instant messaging has replaced not just phone calls but email too. It's value, of course, lies as much in how it enhances the acquiring Facebook as within itself. Shareholder value, then, is about delivering performance today and tomorrow – and in particular your potential for future growth.

Exponential thinking is about thinking big, but it is also about the steps to go from small to big. As Ray Kurzweil said, 'If I were to take 30 linear steps, I'd end up 30 metres away. But what if I said to you take 30 exponential steps … 1, 2, 4, 8, 16, 32, … where would you end up? The answer is a billion metres away, or twenty-six times around the planet.'

The starting point for you as a leader is to take time with your teams to think – how you can create and harness the power of addictive ideas, innovation accelerators and market multipliers. To innovate a better business and to amplify the impact.

10x not 10 per cent … Be inspiring, be exponential!

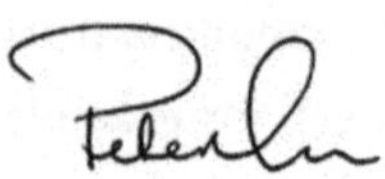

Peter Fisk

Peter Fisk is the founder of GeniusWorks (thegeniusworks.com). He is a professor at Spain's IE Business School. His books include *Gamechangers* (Wiley, 2014). He has been selected on the Thinkers50 Radar as a thinker to watch.

From Marshall Goldsmith

Four Classic Challenges for Smart CEOs

Dear CEO,

In my role as an executive coach, I have had the opportunity to work with over 150 major CEOs. As a group they would score well above the norm on any standard definition of intellectual intelligence (I am not referring to 'emotional intelligence', 'artistic intelligence' or other forms of intelligence).

While we often consider the blessings that come with a high IQ, we seldom think of the challenges that come with extreme intelligence. In this chapter, I will discuss four classic challenges faced by smart CEOs that are even more common among the 'super-smart'.

1. *Proving how smart we are*

For ten years I had the privilege of being on the Board of the Peter Drucker Foundation. This gave me the opportunity to spend over fifty days with the man who was (to me) the greatest management thinker who ever lived.

One of the great lessons Peter taught was:

> Our mission in life is to make a positive difference – not to prove how smart we are.

It is amazing how many leaders fail to grasp this basic lesson.

One of the 'super-smart' leaders that I coached had two simultaneous doctorates from one of the most challenging schools in the world, one in science and one in the humanities – with honours – in five years!

The first time I interviewed him I took copious notes. After an hour I said, 'Dr. Smith, let me read to you the six times in the past hour that you have told me how smart you really were.'

As I read back his verbatim comments, he was embarrassed. 'What an ass!' he said of himself.

I replied, 'You are not an ass. You just have an incredibly high need to prove how smart you are. Perhaps in the future you can cut back on this a little.'

I've given this same advice to lots of smart CEOs!

2. *Proving how right we are*

One night I had dinner with a top four-star general from the US Army. We were surrounded by other 2–4 star generals. The general asked me an interesting question, 'Marshall, who is your favourite customer?'

I replied, 'Sir, my favourite customer is smart, dedicated, driven to achieve, has incredible integrity, gets results – and is a stubborn, opinionated know-it-all who never wants to admit he or she is wrong.'

I looked around the room and asked, 'Do you think any of the generals in this very room may fit such a description?'

He laughed and replied, 'Marshall, we have a target-rich opportunity!'

It is incredibly difficult for super-smart people to hear something that they disagree with without proving the other person is wrong. After all, if others disagree with us, we assume, because we are so smart, they must be wrong. The higher we move up in leadership, the more destructive this habit can become.

3. *I already know that*

It is incredibly difficult for smart people to listen to someone tell us something that we already know without pointing out, 'I already know that.'

Imagine that you are my boss. I am young, dedicated and enthusiastic. I come to you with an idea. You think it is a great idea.

Rather than just saying 'Great idea!' which gives credit to the other person, our tendency is to say, 'That is a great idea, I already knew that!' which gives credit to ourselves.

Next time, just say, 'Great idea!'

4. *Why can't they be me?*

Joe, one of the 'super-smart' leaders that I have coached, had one of the classic challenges faced by the 'super-smart'.

One day, I watched as he led his team meeting. One of his direct reports was clearly having problems meeting goals.

Joe became very frustrated, 'Can't you see how X would help you solve your problem? It seems obvious to me!' He then looked around the table and said, 'I cannot believe that I am the ONLY person in the room who thought of X! What were all of you thinking about?'

After the meeting, I explained to Joe that *they* were not the unusual ones – *he* was! Almost nobody in the world was as smart as he was.

'Super-smart' people can often make connections and see patterns that are not obvious to normal people – or even 'smart' people. In many cases the smarter we are, the more difficult this may be to understand.

Final thought

One of the greatest leaders that I have ever met taught me a wonderful lesson, 'For the great individual *achiever,* it is "all about me". For the great *leader,* it is "all about them"'.

It can be incredibly difficult, and yet it is highly possible, to make the transition from it is 'all about me' – proving I am smart, proving I am right, knowing all of the answers – to it is 'all about them' – proving they are right and being proud of them having the answers.

If you're a super-smart CEO, don't spend your time proving how smart you are, be wise and spend your time helping other people be the heroes.

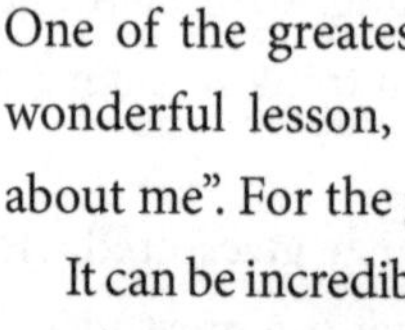

Marshall Goldsmith

Marshall Goldsmith is one of the world's leading executive coaches and author, most recently of *Triggers* (Crown, 2015). He is a Thinkers50 ranked thinker and winner of the 2015 Thinkers50 Leadership Award.

From Hal Gregersen

Dear CEO,

I've been spending a lot of time with CEOs and other enterprise leaders lately, gaining a better grasp of what they see as the hardest part of the job. Across some 200 interviews to date, a clear pattern has emerged. Presiding over vast organizations executing today's strategies, these effective leaders are highly aware that their job is to say when that strategy should change. They must be, more than anyone in the organization, tuned to the signals that disruption is afoot and able to see the opportunities in times of dynamic change. Unfortunately, they also know that – exactly because of their exalted position in the organization – they are especially prone to *missing* those signals. A thick bubble tends to form around the C-Suite, insulating them from challenges to the status quo.

This dilemma is intrinsic to the CEO's job, a built-in design flaw of hierarchies. The good news, however, is that a fair number of the CEOs I've met have taken it on quite directly. These tend, not incidentally, to be the leaders of impressively innovative organizations – people like Daniel Lamarre at Cirque du Soleil, Elon Musk of Tesla and SpaceX, Marc Benioff of Salesforce.com. All have recognized that avoiding the dilemma requires deliberate work to keep pushing themselves beyond their comfort zones.

What's 'comfortable' for a CEO? We all know the habits that allow executives to rise through the ranks and be effective as managers. CEOs are comfortable making decisions with confidence that they are right. They are comfortable giving speeches and generally holding forth about what their people should be focusing on. They are comfortable with delegating – entrusting other people to bring them the information they need in distilled forms that they can process efficiently.

What I'm suggesting, based on what I see the most impressive leaders doing, is that CEOs resolve right now to be less right, less vocal and less comfortable. They – meaning you – must find ways to keep toggling out of transmit mode and into receiving mode. On a day-to-day basis, this is easier said than done.

At Charles Schwab, CEO Walt Bettinger has institutionalized a number of ways to ensure he gets the information the organization might otherwise try to protect him from. 'Brutally Honest Reports' are one mechanism, required monthly from his direct reports (who have cascaded the same practice throughout the company). Ed Catmull at Pixar has institutionalized a 'Brain Trust' of high-level creatives to weigh in on problematic projects. At Aramex, Fadi Ghandour built a culture on his habit of spending time with front-line workers – for instance, by foregoing the limo from the airport and hitching a ride with local Aramex van drivers instead.

These are just a few of many tactics I've heard about from leaders determined to be a little more wrong, a little more quiet, a little more uncomfortable – and therefore a lot more likely to encounter assumption-challenging input. At a high level, these everyday habits have one very big thing in common. They are all geared not to help leaders discover slightly better answers to long-standing questions, but to surface surprisingly new questions that could guide their enterprises' futures. Ask any inventor of a truly novel and dramatically better solution about its genesis. You won't hear about a reengineering of the old offering. You'll hear about a fundamental reframing of the problem. A radical reframing, in fact, where catalytic questions wipe away false assumptions and accelerate rapid transformations down valuable new paths.

A short letter to a CEO doesn't give much space to convey life-changing advice. But this one could be the exception. I'll frame it as a set of questions: what could you start doing today to tear away the insulating layers between you and the ever-changing real world? If you were resolved to prove yourself wrong about something you believe, where might you go and whom might you talk with? And if you don't encourage the question-raising that will unlock future value for your enterprise, who will?

Hal Gregersen

Hal Gregersen is the executive director of the MIT Leadership Center. He is the co-author of *The Innovator's DNA* (HBR, 2011). He is a Thinkers50 ranked thinker.

From Anil Gupta and Haiyan Wang

Dear CEO,

Congratulations on your phenomenal accomplishments as the CEO of Global Solutions Inc. over the last ten years. Relative to the biggest competitors that the company faced in 2006, GSI today is not only the most customer-centric but also among the most cost-efficient. Your products are sold in over 100 countries. You have shifted bulk of the manufacturing operations to China, India and Vietnam. You have doubled the company's R&D budget. Last but not least, you have set up new R&D centres in Beijing and Bangalore, thereby enabling the company to get more mileage for its R&D dollars.

But, that is yesterday's story. Past success is scant guarantee of survival even five years from now. Remember Nokia or Blackberry. Since change occurs exponentially, the drivers of success in every industry are likely to change more dramatically in the next ten years than over the last twenty-five years. The mother of all game changers will be *digital disruption*. It is coming at us with breakneck speed. As is already the case in your industry, the potential disrupters tend to be newcomers with no constraints imposed by legacy investments, legacy business models and legacy mindsets.

If GSI were to be a bit slow in figuring out how to crack Tier 3 and 4 markets in China, the rural market in India or the vast bulk of sub-Saharan Africa, it will hurt but you'll likely have the time to get up and fight another day. However, if you are even 2–3 years late in figuring out how to make digital disruption work for you, you may never recover.

The transformations under way at *The Washington Post* and GE are instructive. Despite the fact that both of these are among the oldest enterprises in the American economy, they are well on the way to becoming the digital leaders within their industries – far ahead of any incumbent or newcomer.

Along with *The New York Times*, the *Post* has been one of America's iconic newspapers with a stellar track record of Pulitzer and other prizes. Yet, as with other newspapers, the Internet hit the *Post* hard. First, it lost classified advertising. Then, it started losing readers to online channels such as BuzzFeed. As the haemorrhaging deepened, the owners responded by shutting down expensive bureaus around the world. By 2012, the *Post* was well on its way to becoming just a local news daily.

Since buying *The Washington Post* from the Graham family in 2013, Jeff Bezos has transformed the media company. It now has twice as many readers, has zoomed past *The New York Times* and is within striking distance of BuzzFeed to become the #1 content channel bar none. Bezos' profound insight, and dictum, has been that the Internet should be viewed not as a challenge but 'as a gift'. This means treating the *Post* as an Internet and mobile media company first, and only secondarily as a print newspaper. Bezos has also infused the *Post* with his well-known tenets such as customer obsession and relentless experimentation.

The strategy around content creation has been turned on its head. Content is now created primarily for the Internet and mobile; a subset of it then finds its way into print. The *Post* now publishes over 1,200 articles per day. Readers are attracted by a mix of breaking news and fun photo slideshows (such as '15 awkward photos of world leaders that explain 2015') and then kept absorbed by in-depth stories such as a multimedia report on the Obama presidency. The *Post*'s content is now distributed over social media such as Facebook and Twitter and, via partnerships, to readers of nearly 100 other newspapers.

GE is a very different type of company. Yet, Jeff Immelt's ongoing transformation of GE is no less profound. The new motto is: 'The digital company. That's also an industrial company.' Immelt has hired the company's first chief digital officer, who lives and works out of Silicon Valley. The company has launched Predix, a software and services platform, with the goal of making it the leader in 'industrial cloud' in the same way that Amazon Web Services has become the leader in 'enterprise cloud'.

GE is also busy installing sensors in the hundreds of thousands of its equipment already installed on customer premises. These sensors enable the company and its customers to leverage the power of big data and machine learning to improve the productivity and reliability of its equipment. In 2015, GE generated over $5 billion in revenue from software and aims to hit $15 billion by 2020.

The take aways for GSI? First, adopt a 'future back' mindset; look at today from the lens of tomorrow rather than the other way around. Second, be proactive in digitizing your products, services and processes relentlessly. Third, think ecosystem rather than enterprise. As with Google's Android, the returns may accrue indirectly rather than directly; Android is free but Google gets a cut of the user's payments for purchases on Android. Fourth, experiment-experiment-experiment. Technologies are evolving rapidly and no company can be smart enough to know in advance all that lies ahead. Last but not least, set up and embrace incubators. The future demands keeping track of and partnering with new ventures created explicitly to disrupt incumbents.

Sincerely,

Anil Gupta and Haiyan Wang

Haiyan Wang is the managing partner of the China India Institute, a Washington DC-based research and consulting organization. She has been shortlisted for Thinkers50 awards and is the co-author (with Anil Gupta) of *The Silk Road Rediscovered* and *Getting China and India Right.*

Anil Gupta holds the Michael D. Dingman Chair in Strategy, Globalization and Entrepreneurship at the Smith School of Business, the University of Maryland at College Park. He also serves as chairman of the China India Institute. He is a Thinkers50 ranked thinker.

From Margaret Heffernan

Dear CEO,

We are where we are. That should be obvious but business leaders are spending a lot of time harkening back to times and conditions long gone. Business moves forward, not back. And right now the big change that you and your peers confront is our increasing inability to predict accurately over any significant timescale.

It used to be – this may be what you learned at business school – that you worked feverishly on a carefully considered, well debated three to five year plan; then the entire company executed furiously to achieve success. But today, if you do that, you will be wasting your time. Your plan would depend on so many risky assumptions as to be pointless; looking out a year or two may be the best you can hope for. That's why the old way of managing won't work any more. It isn't a question of doing it better – but doing something different.

Your challenge now is to build an organization that is adaptive, flexible and febrile in its responsiveness. This will put change programmes into the shade, because your end goal is a culture and structure capable of evolving constantly. You will need people who love learning, can learn (safely) from mistakes and are generous in their support of others. The super-chickens will have to go, however talented they may be.

Your two enemies in this endeavour will be hierarchy and bureaucracy. Hierarchy provides tremendous reassurance but at the cost of accountability: there are always plenty of other people to blame. If the business is carrying risks, or is surrounded by opportunities, you need every single person in your organization to feel responsible for attending to these. Hierarchy provides the perfect excuse to do the opposite, making it more likely that you will learn too late what's going on down there. Moreover, you want people to be able to easily move around the organization – spreading ideas, learning and perspectives – without loss of status. How few layers can you live with?

Too much of the bureaucratic machinery used to run organizations has turned clever, imaginative and independent thinkers into bad robots. Targets and performance management systems reduce both autonomy and accountability: as long as employees do as they've been told, it isn't their fault if it is mad, bad or stupid. So the reassuring machinery of bureaucracy needs to be slimmed down. Focus instead on creating the conditions in which the people can you trust can pursue them the right way. Targets distract and destroy. Well-defined outcomes can liberate.

Your people – the talent – need collectively to look like the markets you serve. To get the most from the intelligence network that is your workforce, gather together different kinds of people with a wide variety of thinking styles and educational backgrounds, give them the courage, freedom and safety to speak up, argue and debate – and then listen to them. Open innovation platforms reveal how much more creative capacity people have than their day jobs allow to surface. Take this as your challenge. Build the connective tissue that allows ideas to spread and improve, the social capital that encourages creative risk taking and collaboration. Most organizations are poor estimators of talent and do best when they raise expectations not of the few but of everyone.

Between your organization and society can be either a wall or a porous membrane. The former may make you feel safe but will always provoke challenges of relevance and legitimacy; walls make innovation harder and wilful blindness easier. A more open relationship to society can keep your organization refreshed, and renewed, sustainably creative and legitimate. That transition, from a closed to an open culture, may be the hardest challenge you face, in yourself and in your organization. But the former will curb growth, while the latter will sustain it.

No one succeeds alone. And, as one board member once told me at the end of a particularly bad quarter: Nobody said it was easy. Leadership is a privilege and sustaining it requires passion for, and attention to, the environment and people that make success possible. When they thrive, you will.

Margaret Heffernan

A former executive, **Margaret Heffernan** is the author of five books: *The Naked Truth: A Working Woman's Manifesto about Business and What Really Matters*, *How She Does It* (published in paperback as *Women on Top*), *Willful Blindness: Why We Ignore the Obvious at our Peril*, *A Bigger Prize: Why Competition Isn't Everything and How We Do Better* and *Beyond Measure*.

Margaret Heffernan

From Linda A. Hill

Dear CEO,

You are being paid to ensure the long-term health of your organization. Not only do you have to build an organization that can execute, you must also build an organization that can innovate – not once, but time and again. Innovation is not just about thriving; in today's economy it is about surviving. For over a decade, my collaborators and I have been studying exceptional leaders of innovation from across the world, in a wide range of industries. What we found may surprise you.

Most leaders, by the time they have made it to the C-Suite, have come to believe that the CEO's primary role is to set the vision and inspire others to fulfil it. While there are times when this notion of leadership is essential – when leading change – it does not work when it comes to building an organization that can routinely innovate. Leading innovation is not about setting direction and saying to your colleagues, 'Follow me'. They don't want to follow you to the future; they want to co-create it with you.

The leaders we studied adopted a broad and inclusive definition of innovation. They believed innovation can be a product, service, business model, process or way of organizing. Innovations can be incremental as well breakthrough. For them, innovation can come from anyone anywhere in the organization. The challenge is to unleash the 'slices of genius' in the organization and harness them for the collective good.

We know from our work and others' that innovation emerges most often from the collaboration of diverse people. Collaboration means far more than a simple willingness to work together. Innovation requires not 'go along to get along' cooperation, but rather, passionate discussion and debate. Innovation thrives on diversity, and a truly original solution to a problem can rarely be reached without the conflict of ideas and opinions, patience to test and learn from multiple approaches and courage to hold options open until they can be integrated into new and useful solutions. Managing the emotions, stress and conflict inherent in this process can make leading innovation uncomfortable and unnatural, even for the most effective leaders. Yet when we studied leaders who had created organizations that could innovate time and again, this is what we saw them do.

How can you do it, you ask? You can start by nurturing three key organizational capabilities that are required for innovative problem-solving: creative abrasion – the ability to generate a robust marketplace of ideas through constructive debate and often conflict; creative agility – the ability to test and refine ideas through rapid experimentation and learning; and creative resolution – the ability to integrate or combine the best aspects of ideas, even ones that seem fundamentally opposable, to reach a superior solution.

Under the best of circumstances, innovation is risky business. Even when it works, the pay-offs are longer term in nature. You cannot do it alone. You will need not only your colleagues, but also your board. In our latest research on boards and innovation, too many CEOs tell us their boards are 'less than friendly' to innovation. Whose fault is that? It is a complicated story. Our advice is: remember, board members are only human. Frankly, it takes courage for them to act in the long-term interests of the organization, while the markets are becoming increasingly short-sighted in orientation. They too are bombarded by activists and other stakeholders who are becoming more assertive in their demands.

When it comes to innovation, board members tell us there can no longer be a bright line between the board and management when shaping innovation strategy. So, you can't afford to keep your board at arms' length in an effort to 'control' the conversation and see your vision realized. Instead, you must build a partnership in which all members of the board are fully engaged. It is this partnership mindset that will allow you to move from a 'tell-sell process' towards a true give-and-take dialogue about the myriad dilemmas inherent to innovation. In short, you need creative abrasion in the boardroom – a capability all too rare today.

As CEO, you can help your board develop a culture of healthy and rigorous debate, both among board members and between the board and management team. You need to be very deliberate in coming up with learning experiences that can give the board insight into your business and the competitive landscape, so they will be prepared to do the risk/reward calculations required. Management must feel safe coming to the board with their innovative ideas – even the 'half-baked' ones; they must be prepared to expect more freewheeling discussion and the provocative and penetrating questions that might emerge. You want the board to become your trusted advisors, your idea-sparring partners. Through support and confrontation, the board can push management's thinking forward and provide a much needed 'reality check'.

Reshaping an 'unfriendly' board into one that is 'friendly to innovation' will take time. As we are learning from our research, changing board culture is tough – but it is work that must be done if your organization is to prosper.

It's time to rethink your leadership mindset when it comes to innovation. Your responsibility to your colleagues and board is not to be the 'solo genius' who drives innovation. Your role is to be the stage-setter for the hard work ahead.

With deepest admiration,

Linda A. Hill

Linda A. Hill is Wallace Brett Donham Professor of Business Administration at Harvard Business School, Faculty Chair of the HBS Leadership Initiative and co-author of *Collective Genius: The Art and Practice of Leading Innovation* (Harvard Business Review Press, 2014). She won the Thinkers50 Innovation Award in 2015.

From Vlatka Hlupic

A Big Change, and an Empowering One

Dear CEO,

Every once in a while, one comes across a major shift in our way of thinking about society: representation by Parliament, for example, and the concept of human rights.

In business management we are on the threshold of a similar, momentous change. For decades now, the dominant approach has been based around the pursuit of short-term financial targets and cost control, with powerful chief executives deploying human resources as they seek to maximize returns. Concerns for welfare, or for society, were assumed to be an optional extra. You were supposed to choose between profits and conscience.

We now know that this approach is seriously flawed – and from a business perspective, as well as from social and environmental considerations. What is interesting is that business leaders are now forming part of a consensus challenging this paradigm; it is not just a few gurus and academics, although it is based on research.

Over the course of the past two years I have had the opportunity to carry out in-depth interviews with senior leaders in the corporate and public sectors. They are now in agreement with thought leaders: something big has to change – a move to humanizing the workplace.

It is a fundamental shift in approach and mindset. For example, traditionally we have placed emotion in opposition to the rational quest to maximize short-term profits. People were called 'resources', and leaders assumed a role of command and control, managing to targets and saying 'just get it done'. What we have learned is that this doesn't maximize profits – or even control. Such an approach leads to frustration and unintended consequences. It can hamper the ability to serve the customer and generate returns.

The emerging consensus is that we need to harness human emotion, rather than block it; to inspire, rather than command. This is not a utopian idea; it is how the best performing companies already operate. It will explain the difference between those parts of your business that are really delivering and those that are getting stuck. Once the energy of your people is unleashed, the customers get a great service and profits take care of themselves.

In the detail of some of the research, we have found that the question of mindset is actually very powerful. All the matters that used to be dismissed as the 'soft stuff' – values, culture, mindset, behaviour – is actually the fuel. In research, we have been able to identify specific power levers that help us move up from mediocre to high performance. We move up from a climate of fear and ignorance, to concern for the common good; this change can be effected by the right style of leadership.

The implications for business leadership and organizational design are immense. Priorities are turned upside down, as we elevate of the importance of leadership behaviour and surveys on employees' mindset and engagement. Scarcely any part of the business model will escape an overhaul.

As I mentioned, this is not utopia. Difficult decisions will still have to be made; budgets cannot always be increased, some product lines will have to be closed and some positions made redundant. But what we have learned is that the organizations with high trust and performance make such changes more effectively than others, with fewer redundancies and less of a dip in performance. Cost control is still important, but it can become easier with high engagement. One of the business leaders who is overseeing a transformation from a bureaucratic to an entrepreneurial culture in a large European company said to me:

> This is not a New Age kind of leadership … And I'm not doing this because it's fun. I'm doing this because it's important. I'm doing it because this is the only way to get results. This is about changing a culture.

This historic shift in the business model is daunting, but it is also tremendously exciting. No longer do we have to sacrifice conscience in the pursuit of profit. You can do well and do good; you can even do well *by* doing good. Your people are not your resources, but your partners, in a humanized, enlightened workplace.

Let's make the future happen now.

Vlatka Hlupic

Vlatka Hlupic is the author of *The Management Shift – How to Harness the Power of People and Transform Your Organization for Sustainable Success* (Palgrave Macmillan, 2014). She is Professor of Business and Management at the University of Westminster.

From Whitney Johnson

To Whom It Should Concern – the Chief Executive Officer

I talk about disruption and disruptors. For a lot of people, the term 'disruption' is heard commonly enough that they tune it out as a mere buzzword. This is unfortunate, because disruption is a powerful force that transforms organizations, communities and ultimately the world. It's critical to the success of your organization, but the tricky secret is that companies and organization don't disrupt unless their people do.

According to Towers Perrin, Intl., organizations with a highly engaged workforce increased operating income by 19.2 per cent, while low engagement led to a 32.7 per cent decline in operating profits.

That's the good news.

The bad news is that the data on employee engagement is abysmal. Really, really bad. You may think that your biggest problem is something happening at the government policy level, or systemic flaws in your business or financial model that must be addressed, or the latest tricks your competitors are getting up to. The reality is, your biggest problem is that your employees are disengaged from their work and from the mission of your enterprise. In fact, if they're like the majority of American workers, the phrase 'bored out of their gourd' aptly describes how your average employee feels while on the job. For you.

The famous annual Gallup poll on employee engagement hasn't reported much change in several years. The fraction of employees who feel engaged at work has hovered stubbornly just below one-third. Fifty per cent say they are 'not engaged' and over 17 per cent unabashedly describe themselves as 'actively disengaged'. I suspect that means they're hunting for a new job, and if they are bright, talented and capable they will find one and with it, hopefully, a better chance to strut their stuff than is currently available to them. They will disrupt themselves. But even the merely disengaged are less productive, have little motivation or outlet for their gifts and are contributing less to your bottom line than you might wish. Disengagement is highest among the younger generations of workers – the most innovative, tech savvy and frustratingly mobile members of the workforce. These valuable and expensive resources will be out your door as well, in less than three years on average.

Your workplace culture almost certainly needs to change to encourage and facilitate internal personal disruption and you must lead the charge. Here's what I recommend, to start:

Develop managers as talent spotters to identify the potential value of disruptive employees, clear their path and green-light their dreaming and innovation. Speed new ideas on to realization. Watch out for the nay-sayers, those who throw up obstacles to change. Adopt the mindset of a cycling team, with everyone helping the fittest riders move into the lead.

Cultivate a risky playing field, where failure is not terminal and employees can explore possibilities, venture into untried territory and learn from mistakes as well as successes. Real stretch assignments + real accountability = real progress.

Reward talent-developers. Which of your many managers are willing to truly encourage the people who could replace them? Who has a lot of subordinates promoted from their department or is willing to broker moves for them? Managers add value by developing nascent talent and they build morale and momentum by helping employees disrupt themselves internally.

Provide genuine and tangible remuneration for those who bring their distinctive strengths to work for you. Personal disruptors should be celebrated and rewarded with open doors to additional innovation.

Train to train, not to retain. Make opportunities to learn a do more the modus operandi rather than a tactic of last resort to placate disgruntled high value employees. Those who know they are being groomed for additional responsibilities are more likely to hang around and embrace new challenges.

Think long term and ride out the near term productivity setbacks that can occur when employees take on new roles. Change brings growing pains, but growing pains are a desirable problem, unlike the acute discomforts that accompany ossification and degeneration.

Engagement. Loyalty. Innovation. Higher performance. Higher profits. These are impressive outcomes that result from one simple input – encouraging personal disruption. It is going to happen no matter what you do. The only question is whether your valuable employees disrupt *for* you or *from* you. Help your employees achieve their dreams while on the job for you and the dreams you hold for your business are more likely to come true as well.

Wishing you every success as YOU personally disrupt your status quo,

Whitney Johnson

Whitney Johnson began working as a secretary on Wall Street. She eventually became a successful investment banker. This experience was the foundation of her first best-seller, *Dare, Dream, Do.* She went on to become president and co-founder of Rose Park Advisors' Disruptive Innovation Fund with Clayton Christensen. Most recently, Johnson has developed her ideas in *Disrupt Yourself: Putting the Power of Disruptive Innovation to Work* (Routledge, 2015).

Whitney Johnson is also co-founder of Forty Women over 40 to Watch and a fellow at the Tribeca Disruptive Innovation Awards. She is a Thinkers50 ranked thinker.

From Soren Kaplan

Dear CEO,

This letter is an appeal to you to take action – to do the one and only thing that can save your company, preserve your employees' jobs and continue providing value to your customers, your suppliers, your community and the world.

As you've experienced recently, competitive advantage no longer exists. Today's success factors become tomorrow's vulnerabilities. The ability to survive – and thrive – relies on how adeptly you can steer your organization in the direction of opportunity and away from obsolescence.

In your last earnings call, you proclaimed the importance of balancing quarterly results with long-term investment and growth. You said your success metrics included triple bottom line measures that embraced people, the planet and profit. These are great aspirations.

But here's the problem: *Unless you've discovered that elusive magic formula that will give you an unlimited growth trajectory into the indefinite future, all of this will be impossible to achieve.*

There is only one way to do it. You must create a culture of innovation that becomes your *invisible advantage* – an environment that promotes freethinking, an entrepreneurial spirit and sustainable value creation across all levels and across all functions. This ultimate source of competitive advantage lies beneath the surface of what your competitors can see. Your invisible advantage includes the unwritten rules, values and assumptions that influence the behaviour to drive innovation. That's the only thing that will consistently help you achieve your triple bottom line metrics and grow the business into the foreseeable future.

Of course, the biggest problem with this is that there's no 'best practice' to create and sustain a culture of innovation since every organization is different. So, you have a choice. You can decide to let your culture run itself, which may or may not produce your magic formula for the future. Or, you can take steps to shape your culture towards an environment that promotes incremental innovation everywhere, major advancements that push the core business forward and even disruptive innovations that change the game.

Here's the good news. By understanding the things that shape norms, values and behaviour, it becomes possible to influence them – and to create a culture of innovation.

Through many years of research and experience, I'll leave you with five principles and practices that you can begin to apply today to create your invisible advantage:

1. ***Be intentional with your innovation intent*** – Your corporate vision sounds alarmingly like everyone else's vision: become the #1 provider of blah, blah, blah. Another problem is that your leadership incessantly talks about creating shareholder value. Few people are truly motivated to get up in the morning to help shareholders increase value. Increasing shareholder value might be the result of innovation, but it's not what motivates most

people to give it their all over the long term. Instead, create your innovation intent by framing the way you want to change the world, and make your intent about the customer.

2. ***Make 'innovation' everyone's job*** – It's no secret the business world has become enamored by 'disruptive' innovation. Everyone wants to be the next Apple, Uber or Airbnb. Nothing wrong with that! But recognizing that innovation comes in different sizes – incremental improvements, major advancements to the core business and big disruptions that reinvents the industry – helps demystify the whole concept of innovation. Promote the fact that innovation isn't just about technology, products or services – it's also about processes, partnerships, capability building and business models. Build innovation into everyone's job description to ensure innovation is embraced by each and every employee, no matter their role or function.
3. ***Step in, then step back*** – Telling employees to 'go forth and innovate' isn't enough. With the premise that everyone has an equal opportunity to add new forms of value, it's essential to help jump-start the process. Create an innovation toolkit that lays out the principles and practices of the innovation process. Don't over-structure the approach. Provide people with opportunities like workshops and hackathons to focus on real challenges and opportunities in a 'safe' environment. Give everyone in the organization the time and means to innovate,

and then leave them alone. Give them a simple way to generate, test, develop and fund ideas.

4. ***Measure what's meaningful*** – Management guru Peter Drucker once said, 'What's measured improves.' Said another way: you get what you measure. Take a look at your metrics and see which measures stifle versus promote innovation. Start measuring things at a higher level than individual P&L's since the game-changers are more likely to occur through collaboration and within the 'white space' that sits between business units. Go beyond financial metrics and start measuring the company's ability to enter new markets or create new business models.
5. ***Curate cultural symbols*** – Everything your leaders do communicates what's important and valued by your organization. Symbols represent the invisible operating assumptions of an organization, and they come in many forms – values, awards, success stories, catch phrases, acronyms and even facial expressions. You have a choice: you can let symbols like your assigned parking spots for high level managers to communicate the value of hierarchy (which stifles innovation) or you can choose to create innovation awards, profile your 'intrapreneurs' through company-wide storytelling and brand your innovation efforts in ways that reinforce the value and importance of invention and reinvention across all levels and functions.

The soft stuff is the hardest stuff for competitors to copy. And the future's only sustainable competitive advantage lies in creating an environment where innovation becomes the operating norm. Build your invisible advantage and you won't just survive in our increasingly disruptive world, you'll thrive.

Best regards,

Soren Kaplan

Soren Kaplan (sorenkaplan.com) is the author of *Leapfrogging* and *The Invisible Advantage* (Greenleaf, 2017). A former Silicon Valley executive, he is an affiliated professor at the Center for Effective Organizations at the University of Southern California.

From Martin Lindstrom

Instinct: The Most Important Leadership Skill of Tomorrow

Dear CEO,

Some years ago, while driving from Poland to Vienna, my GPS broke down. Forget about buying a printed map. They'd vanished in the two decades since I'd last looked for one. My navigational skills are questionable and I'd only been in the area once before, but I had no choice other than to point the car in what I guessed was the right direction and simply drive. Remarkably, I arrived at my destination without a single wrong turn. When I puzzled over how I'd managed, I could only come up with one conclusion: I had allowed my instincts to run the show.

I define an instinct as an accumulation of insights obtained though decades of experiences, all guiding the seeker to an answer. An instinct is the art of connecting thousands of impressions. One can't consciously explain how all those dots were connected. They simply were.

Some of the most powerful business leaders of all time share one thing. They trust in their instincts. One example is Rupert Murdoch, who supposedly reads most of his newspapers every morning. That adds up to more than fifty newspapers every morning. If a headline is out of line with what he believes his readers want, he's on the phone to his editors. He has the knack of putting himself in his reader's shoes, whether it's a business reader of the *Wall Street Journal*, a worker reading the *New York Post*, or a British housewife reading *The Sun*.

The founder of IKEA was no different. You'd find Ingvar Kamprad running cash registers in his stores. Why? Because he was determined to understand not just *what* people buy, but also *why*. Sitting at the checkout stand let him interact with customers, one at a time.

'There is only one boss', said Sam Walton, founder of Walmart. 'The customer. And he can fire everybody in the company, from the chairman on down, simply by spending his money somewhere else.' You'd often find Walton walking around his stores, interacting with customers.

Last year, NBC asked me to turn around a range of small businesses across North America for their Today Show. I quickly realized that these businesses shared one problem: a serious disconnect with the consumer. Time after time, owners viewed their businesses from their own perspective, rather than from the consumer's viewpoint.

One of the retailers was a 100-year-old shop named Veach's Toy Station. As I entered their store, their lack of customer focus struck me instantly. So, I lined up the entire staff and asked them to join me on our hands and knees to crawl through the store. I wanted them to see the world from a six-year-old's perspective. 'Can you reach that toy?' I asked. 'Can you see that doll? Can you play with that car?' They answered, *No, of course not*. But wasn't their primary consumer a child below the age of ten?

I'm reminded of the late Michele Ferrero, Italy's richest man, and owner of Nutella, Kinder Surprise, Ferrero Rocher and Tic Tac. Some years ago, Ferrero was spotted on all fours, crawling through a retail store to test whether children could reach his chocolates.

Leaving the office and entering the world of consumers can be uncomfortable. Suddenly, you're stripped of your expensive tie, your name tag and your flashy watch – all those things that contribute to your image. As you join your consumers in your shop aisles, or even in their homes, you become an ordinary person. But how can you know how your consumer thinks if you never stand in her shoes? Remember my definition about instinct as an accumulation of thousands of observations? Isn't that the secret of Murdoch, Kamprad, Walton and Ferrero?

I will argue, strongly, that a successful organization can't be run on Big Data alone. After all, your competition has all the same data that you have, and it will lead them to the same conclusions.

Data doesn't create meaning. We do. The executive needs to be far more than a data analyst. He should constantly strive to see the world from a customer's point of view. I believe that the truly dynamic business leader of the future, though immersed in a flood of Big Data, will need the courage to adapt the mindset of the consumer. He must dare to trust his instincts.

Martin Lindstrom

Martin Lindstrom is author of *Buyology* and *Small Data: The Tiny Clues That Uncover Huge Trends* (www.martinlindstrom.com/smalldata). His books have been translated into forty-seven languages. He was named one of *TIME* magazine's 100 most influential people in the world and has been ranked the world's #1 branding expert for three consecutive years. Lindstrom currently hosts *Main Street Makeover*, a series on NBC's TODAY. He is a Thinkers50 ranked thinker.

From Chengwei Liu

Dear CEO,

You are leading one of the most successful corporations of our time. But I study how great companies fail. One shared feature of the failed companies I studied is that their leaders could not overcome some systematic biases in their decision-making. Worse, they were overconfident in their decisions and their errors are not challenged. Here are three tips for helping you to learn from three damaging mistakes they made for improving your decisions.

First, **be cautious about ideas or candidates with unanimous support**. We like consensus, but ancient Jews knew that if a suspect on trial was unanimously found guilty by all judges, then the suspect was likely to be innocent and will be acquitted because unanimous support indicates that there must remain some form of undiscovered exculpatory evidence. Given that everyone has their own preference and bias, unanimous support is too good to be true and likely to indicate hidden processes such as the candidates are good at politicking and compromising than making important, difficult choices. Or, unanimous support can signal that your employees or top management team are too similar-minded. Overcome your **consensus bias** and choose an idea or appoint someone against unanimity (or even hated by your colleagues) – these wildcards are likely to be opposed or hated for good reasons and can shake things up.

Second, **demote your best executives before succession**. A great Chinese emperor sent his best chancellors to prison for trivial causes before his death. The reason was to protect them from the political conflicts during succession and to give the young emperor a chance to gain the loyalty of these seasoned chancellors by promoting them after the succession. This was a difficult decision because most people thought the emperor had lost his mind. To ensure your successor has the best executives, particularly those who lost in the successor competition, leaders can learn from the old Chinese emperor. The challenge is to overcome your **ego bias** – your decision will be ridiculed, but it is likely to be good for your successor and the longevity of your company.

Third, **attributing your successes to luck to get lucky**. You are already successful. Most people intuitively believe you must have done something right to deserve your successes. Attributing your successes to skill and hard work publicly does not strengthen others' favourable attributions about you. In fact, research shows that attributing successes to own skill and effort will make one look self-serving, arrogant, narcissistic and untrustworthy. Why not take advantage of others' predictable attribution tendencies and attribute your successes to luck instead? Acknowledging luck does not make you look weak. Rather, people will continue believing that you deserved your successes. They will also consider you as modest and trustworthy when you say you were lucky. Exploiting others' **success bias** can even get you luckier – people with new ideas and opportunities will likely choose you and your company as collaborator when your competitors' CEOs fail to overcome their luck bias.

Consensus bias, ego bias and success bias are just three of the biases that hurt important decisions such as innovation, leadership succession and stakeholder management. My work on leader decision-making outlines systematic ways to 'strategize with biases' for improving decisions and sustainable performances. I look forward to working with you and your team!

Yours faithfully,

劉正威

Chengwei Liu

Originally from Taiwan, **Chengwei Liu** is now an associate professor of Strategy and Behavioural Science at Warwick Business School. He was selected as a thinker to watch in the 2016 Thinkers50 Radar.

From Costas Markides

Maximizing Shareholder Value Is the Wrong Thing to be Pursuing

Dear CEO,

Any CEO of a publicly traded company is under intense pressure to maximize shareholder value. This has always been the case but it has become increasingly so in the last few years as a result of more aggressive and impatient investors as well as more data availability and accounting transparency. The need to do this every year – or every quarter – hangs over the head of every CEO like the 'sword of Damocles'. Fail to deliver for a quarter or two and you'd better start looking for a new job! Yet, for any CEO aspiring for success, this is exactly the wrong thing to be pursuing. It is important to understand why.

For his PhD thesis at Harvard, Clark Gilbert tried to understand why some newspaper companies were successful in responding to the Internet, while others failed. He found that those companies that viewed the Internet as a *threat* ended up failing in their response. This is because looking at something as a threat has certain benefits (i.e. it creates the required urgency for action) but it also has costs – our actions tend to be short-term and reactive. Surprisingly, those that viewed the Internet as an *opportunity* also failed in their response. This is because viewing something as an opportunity has certain benefits (i.e. we look at things in a strategic way and take a long-term perspective) but it also has costs – there is no urgency for action. What Gilbert found was that those companies that succeeded in their response to the Internet approached the Internet as *both* a threat *and* an opportunity: (http://hbswk.hbs.edu/item/2967.html). Doing so allowed them not only to create the sense of urgency required to generate action but also to tackle the task strategically and proactively.

This is just one of the *many* studies available which show that **how we view or frame something can have a big impact on what we do** (and how successful we are in our actions). And that is why it makes a big difference how we frame one of the key issues facing the modern corporation, namely: 'what is the goal or purpose of the modern corporation?'

One view – favoured by the financial markets – is that the purpose of the modern corporation is to maximize shareholder value. Another view, coming primarily from people in strategy is that the purpose of business is *not* to maximize shareholder value. Instead, it is to create great products and services that satisfy customers' needs and in the process improve the state of our world. The argument is that if we focus our attention on creating superb products and services that the world needs, then *as a by-product of that*, we will also maximize profits. Thus, maximizing profits is *not* an end in itself – it is a by-product of something else. Look, for example, at Steve Jobs. He is the one CEO that created more value for shareholders than anybody else. Yet, he never once said that his goal is to maximize shareholder value. No. What he aimed to achieve was radical new products that made our life better. As a result, we bought his products. As a result, he made a lot of money.

People from the financial world usually respond to such arguments by suggesting that while they accept the need to produce superb products and services, this should not be the focus of the corporation. Instead, it should be a by-product of something else. Specifically, they propose that the modern corporation should focus on maximizing shareholder value and as by-product of this we will produce superb products and services. So the essence of the disagreement boils down to this – do we focus on producing superb products and services and as a by-product of this maximize shareholder value? Or do we focus on maximizing shareholder value and as a by-product of this produce superb products and services?

The difference may appear academic but as Gilbert's research demonstrated, how you frame something has a big impact on what people do. So the question we need to ask ourselves is the following: 'If we frame the goal of business as maximizing shareholder value, can we see managers doing things that may maximize shareholder value which are at the same time unethical and/or illegal' (such as selling unnecessary products – say financial derivatives – to uninformed customers)? The answer to this is yes! By contrast, 'if we frame the goal of business as producing superb products and services that make the world a better place, can we see managers doing illegal and unethical things in an effort to achieve this?' It's hard to see how!

And that is why it is important that we win the debate on what the purpose of business really is. It is not to maximize shareholder value but to make the world a better place for everybody (through its products and services). That has always been the purpose of business but somehow we lost sight of it along the way. If we put this goal at the forefront of business, then we will succeed in focusing the attention of millions on what matters most – improving the state of our world for everybody.

Costas Markides

Professor of Strategy and Entrepreneurship at London Business School, **Costas Markides** is the author of *All the Right Moves*, *Fast Second* (with Paul Geroski) and *Game-Changing Strategies* (Jossey Bass, 2008). He has been included in the Thinkers50 ranking on five occasions.

From Roger L. Martin

Dear CEO,

The most pressing challenge facing the CEOs of today's corporations is the incursion into corporate decision-making of data analytics, commonly referred to by the fashionable moniker 'big data'. The state of play is that data analytics is considered fully above reproach: something that modern CEOs simply must embrace. If a CEO doesn't show unqualified reverence for data analytics, it is assumed that the CEO is a Neanderthal and/or Luddite. What has changed is that data analytics has migrated from the fringes of CEO life to the very epicentre. It is now the hottest thing in business.

CEOs are increasingly faced with an endless string of well-meaning but unreflective data analytics enthusiasts telling them that the 'data prove that *X* is true' or the 'correct decision based on the data analytics is to do *Y*'. The absolutely dominant prevailing wisdom is that CEOs should thank the messenger profusely and affirm that the decision based on data analytics is right. Instead, CEOs should instead ask the messenger the following five questions:

1. Question: From what era does all data in the world come?
   Answer: From the past. There is no data about the future – yet.

2. Question: What is the full extent of what data analytics tell us?
   Answer: What has been operative in the past based on how the world has worked in the past.

3. What is our implicit assumption each and every time we use data analytics to decide what to do going forward?
   Answer: We implicitly assume that the future will be a direct extrapolation of the past. It will be either identical to the past or an extrapolation of the observed past trend into the future.

4. What is the probability of making choices to create a future that is different from the past using data analytics?
   Answer: Zero. Data analytics has zero ability to chart out a course that is anything other than an extrapolation of the past into the future.

5. What is the probability that making a choice about the future based on data analytics will turn out badly?
   Answer: High. Last time I checked, frequently the future turns out to be unexpectedly different from the past – annoyingly so, in fact.

The strong likelihood is that the big data enthusiast will not be able to answer any of the five questions, be baffled by the nature of the questions and declare the CEO to be 'anti-analytics'. But by asking the questions and insisting on answers that demonstrate that data analytics are appropriate for the situation in question – and data analytics is appropriate when the future is likely to mirror the past – the CEO will be saving their companies from the modern-day vandals.

Instead, CEOs need to use the only methodology that has ever been useful in making decisions about the future: first, imagine possibilities and second, pick the one for which the most compelling argument can be made. In deciding which is backed by the most compelling argument, CEOs should indeed take into account all data that can be crunched. But in addition, CEOs should also use imagination, judgement and experience of numerous data points from the past that the data analysts wouldn't consider 'objective data' to decide in what way to shape the future – like all the great CEOs in the history of business have done.

In doing so, CEOs will have to accept widespread ridicule in their organizations among the legion of big data enthusiasts, who will say that their CEO lacks rigour and makes decisions on 'gut feel' and is 'old school'. But these enthusiasts are likely to be blind and to have never asked questions concerning the logical limits of their methodology. So CEOs need to stand strong and make decisions that can create a better future for their organization and for humanity.

Sincerely,

Roger L. Martin

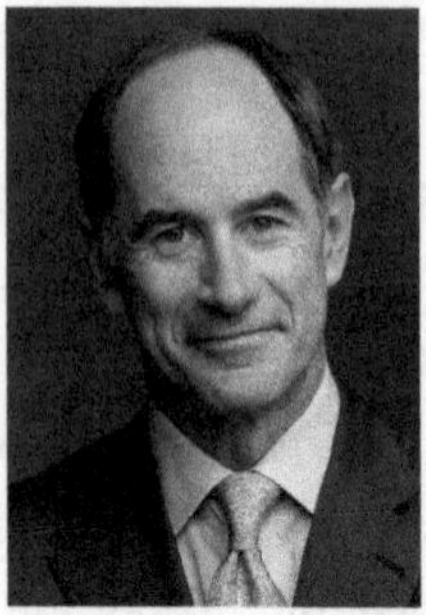

Winner of the Thinkers50 Awards for Best Book and Social Enterprise, **Roger L. Martin** is one of the world's leading authorities on innovation and strategy. His books include *Playing to Win* (with AG Lafley, Procter & Gamble CEO); *The Opposable Mind*; *The Design of Business*; and *Fixing the Game* and *Getting Beyond Better: How Social Entrepreneurship Works* (with Sally Osberg, HBR Press, 2015). Martin is the former dean of the Rotman School of Management at the University of Toronto (where he now holds Premier's Chair in Productivity and Competitiveness).

From Margarita Mayo

Dear CEO,

I've been reflecting on the role of leaders in business and I am encouraged by the many stories I've heard from a variety of leaders, whether they are CEOs of multinationals or start-up founders. However, while we all share a positive motivation, I suspect the job of the CEO today and beyond will be challenging.

If you are like me, you are probably shocked and disheartened by the number of cases of corruption and unethical behaviour and how they have contributed to a crisis in leadership. As a result, the business world has become more sceptical of formal rules and increasingly reliant on personal relationships.

In my view, the most pressing challenge facing you as a CEO today is how to gain back this respect and trust in leadership. I want to talk to you openly about this.

We have a workforce that distrusts leaders. In Edelman's 2015 *Trust Barometer* survey across twenty-seven countries, respondents reported trust levels in business leaders at 43 per cent, a decline of nine points with respect to 2011. 'We see an evaporation of trust', observes Richard Edelman; 'academics, industry and technical experts remain the most credible spokespeople for business, in stark contrast to CEOs'. After all, it wasn't the financial crisis that caused us to lose faith in leaders; rather it was the leaders' own overly hands-off attitude that led people to scepticism.

A generational shift has reinforced the need for authenticity in CEOs. Millennials (born 1980–2000) trust a CEO whom they see as authentic and in touch with his/her inner values. If you are a CEO looking for success with the new workforce, you'd better provide more than a pay cheque. You may wonder whether your authenticity can make you vulnerable in their eyes. The truth is that being authentic makes you stronger and more influential, especially with the new workforce.

It's no exaggeration to say that there is a fundamental change in the role of leaders in this time of disbelief. Leaders are the common glue of our companies and the fabric of our society. Once, leaders based their trust on formal positions, but today they must rely on authentic relationships.

So let's face it; it's necessary to change how you view your role as a leader. I think you should move away from managing *transactional* relationships and invest more time in building *authentic* relationships. And there is an immediacy to this. If you don't act quickly, you risk ineffectiveness – within your company and the world.

So, how can you make such a leadership shift?

I'm not advocating that you simply copy the style of other great leaders. Rather, I'm talking about looking *inside* yourself to discover the heart of your authentic style and then using your passion to motivate your employees. Furthermore, you should be looking *outward* for feedback to reinvent yourself and learn new habits, and looking *after* your employees to enrich their habitat so that they can shine. I think of this as the '3 H's of Authentic Leadership': Heart, Habits and Habitat.

To inspire people to follow you, you have to look first at your **heart**. I think embracing your personal story, both errors and success of your journey, will take you a long way towards an uplifting mission – something more than just a slogan on a wall. Only you can decide what your passion is, but once you do, it is contagious.

It's important to also revisit the logic that authentic leaders must be fixed in their ideas. Consistency can sometimes prevent you and your company from growth and success, especially given the current pace of change. I'm not suggesting that you abandon your core values. But I do think you should continually evolve, stay flexible and reassess your goals and the company's vision. You need to seek out honest feedback and learn new habits.

But it is more than that. It's important to consider the following: How do I want to be remembered twenty years from now? To have a positive lasting influence, you have to create a habitat for employees to grow. If you adopt the type of leadership I'm suggesting you embrace with your employees, not only you will greatly improve the quality of your relationships with them. You'll also have a workforce that is more committed to your vision and contributes to the competitiveness of the company in the long run. And you'll be remembered even when you are no longer here.

To sum up, remember that to become an authentic leader you don't need to fall into the mentality of a super-hero. Instead, shift to the mindset of unsung heroes: Follow your heart and be a passionate actor; be an avid learner – setting new habits to better yourself, but stay humble and grounded; and enrich your habitat to become a chief builder of organizations to live beyond your time.

Yours sincerely,

Margarita Mayo

Margarita Mayo (margaritamayo.com) is Professor of Leadership and Organizational Behavior at IE Business School in Madrid and a Visiting Professor at ESMT – the European School of Management and Technology in Berlin. She is a regular contributor to the *Harvard Business Review* and a Fulbright Alumni of Harvard University.

From Liz Mellon

Dear CEO,

I doubt you remember me. We have met, twice, at one of those breakfasts you hold for high potential talent. I thought I'd just drop you a note to let you know how I'm getting on. I must confess that I found the discipline of work hard to start with, after the carefree days of being a student. But, at the same time, it was a lot of fun. My year's intake was great and we all got along well; you know how that just happens sometimes? Twelve years in and I'm still here and loving it, but something strange happened along the way. I'm the only woman left in my group of talent, among all the men. To be honest, it's getting a bit like that everywhere at work now that I'm an executive.

Yesterday I was in a meeting and I was the only woman. I can remember my mum telling me a funny story about how she was once mistaken at work for a secretary and asked to make the coffee (she's a High Court Judge today). Yesterday I found out that it isn't nearly as funny when it happens to you. Thirty years on! You've got to be kidding, right?! So I did a bit of a tally. Martha left because her boss, who was all outwardly 'diversity rocks!', turned out to be the biggest misogynist since Genghis Kahn. Aurelia was posted to Switzerland, where the schools send the kids home for lunch, so she ran out of energy running to and from work for the lunch hour. I thought Hanna was holding her own as the only woman on her regional team, and she really tried to join in, but finally the endless teambuilding events featuring rock-climbing, pub crawls and football matches just ground her down. Ditto Rebecca, except with her, she was somehow expected to be the team's mum and she got really tired of all the hand-holding and listening. Not her core strength! Sophie wasn't allowed to go part-time and Alexis went on maternity leave and mysteriously failed to return (something about her job being made redundant? Or maybe she just liked being at home. The rumour mill went into overdrive on that one). Alison kept pushing for promotion and was eventually told that she was too demanding, so she left to set up her own business. Suzanne – well you know what the culture's like in development, everyone trying to outdo each other and compete for everything, from who works the longest hours to who ate the latest lunch – exhausting! She was tired of getting feedback telling her that she wasn't 'strong' enough, when her results were in the top five. Cathryn was really pleased when she went to work for a female boss and was excited to have a role model she could emulate. Sadly, her boss loved being the only woman in the room and Cathryn was sidelined until she gave up and left. Oh, and Jane was complimented by her male boss on wearing black, because that made her 'less distracting' – you can't really respect someone after a remark like that, can you?

So I do have a question for you. What can we do now? We've tried fixing the women, we've tried fixing the men and we've tried fixing the culture. Given that what gets measured, gets done, should we set quotas to push us over the line? I'm still here and I want to stay and I want to do well. I know that women make up just over half of humankind and I know that we make the majority of household purchasing decisions, even for goods where you'd think men might take the lead, like cars. So surely, should our company's executives represent the same mix as we find among our customers? All I know is that it was a lot more fun in the old days, when our talent group met up. Honestly, I made excuses to miss the last get-together, because I feel increasingly like an outsider in the group.

When my mum told me stories about trying to be one of the boys (she used to wear trouser suits with ties and stay as late at the bar as any of them), I thought it was hilarious. Quaint. Historically amusing. But to be honest, I'm getting a bit worried that not as much has changed as I had thought. You're a woman, how did you make it?

Yours sincerely

Liz Mellon

Liz Mellon (lizmellon.com) founded Duke Corporate Education in London in 2000 and later served as Regional Managing Director India. Before joining Duke, she was professor of organizational behaviour at London Business School. She is the author of *Inside the Leader's Mind* (FT/Prentice Hall, 2011), chair of the Editorial Board of *Dialogue*, Duke CE's global journal and Executive Director of *Authentic Leadership*. She was included in the Thinkers50 Radar for 2016 and has been previously shortlisted for the Thinkers50 Leadership Award.

From Nilofer Merchant

Challenging Our Definition of Who Is Talented

Dear CEO,

Is there any question that talent matters?

After all, our modern economy is fuelled by the creativity of our people, by the ideas they can come up with and the experiences they provide customers. We all remember Jim Collins, the management guru, saying that we need to get talented people on the bus. Tom Peters called this the age of talent. And without knowing who else and what else is being published in this book you're reading right now, I would bet a bunch of us are saying to you how crucial talent is.

But before we can talk to the talent idea very deeply, can I ask you to stop for a second, and ask yourself, what is it that defines talent to you?

- Is it the person who has honed their skills, and developed the proven expertise?
- Is it the person who is equal to the task?
- Is it the person who persevered and got the education necessary despite the odds?

- Take a few seconds and write it down … What is talent to you?
- ___________________

If you're like a lot of people I've worked with in my corporate career – which has included companies like Apple and Autodesk, from roles ranging from administrative assistant to corporate board member – your notion of talent will find some form of naming the 'right' talent.

Talent, if it is 'right' will have some combination of expertise, proficiency and mastery.

And this is the problem. This definition is too small.

For example, it would preclude the administrative assistant who doesn't have a degree and isn't an expert on your product or service but rather takes calls once in a while from disgruntled customers. This person likely wouldn't have the rank or authority within your firm but could have a key insight into what is needed to do better.

It might preclude those who could shape your market. It might preclude, for example, the teenager whose friend's brother died of a pancreatic cancer disease and who desperately seeks a cure as he channels his grief. The librarian who first deals with him says he is 'too young to know', yet this young man, Jack Andrada, ends up designing a sensor that detects pancreatic cancer 168 times faster than current tests. It's also 90 per cent accurate, 400 times more sensitive and 26,000 times less expensive than existing methods. This person wouldn't have the required credentials or experience necessary to contribute. Yet, he does.

And, it would also preclude anyone who doesn't seem equal to the task. It would rule out the deaf person from, say, … designing speech technologies. The Soviet Union once restricted the deaf from admission to state universities yet Dimitri Kanevsky ends up petitioning to do so, and ultimately has 100 patents to his name as he's a leading expert in speech recognition.

By all standards, these are stories of inherent talent manifest. But, they made it despite the odds of them making it. That's because of the too-small definition of talent. Rather, ideas are often ruled out by who brings them. Judged first by how *qualified* or *right* the 'talent' is that brings those ideas.

So what should be on the top of your agenda?

You must understand how to enable original ideas to surface.

Let's agree that *anyone* – without preapproval or vetting or criteria – can create and contribute. This idea of inclusion is essential for solving new problems as well as for finding new solutions to old problems. The element starts with celebrating each human and, more specifically, something termed *onlyness.*

Onlyness recognizes that each of us is standing in a spot only one stands in, a spot that no one else occupies. It is a function of history and experiences, visions and hopes. That unique point of view is the genesis of new ideas, the ones that challenge the status quo, or improve upon the existing condition. Thus, original ideas come from onlyness. And it's not that everyone *will* have ideas to contribute, but anyone *can.*

The more traditional formulation of the source of ideas was 'talent', but that framework was 'right talent' and thus too often credential-dependent. For a long time, workplaces have relied on gates to show who could contribute because it was a cost-effective method. But it often measured the wrong things. For example, research consistently shows that SAT scores are more a function of socio-economic background than talent. Yet, SAT scores often serve as the gateway to advanced education, to the networks gained in those institutions…. Likely, where you met your friends, where you hire people that you trust. But actual capability can come from anywhere, because each of us is standing in a spot no one else stands in, a function of our history and experiences, visions and hopes. And from that place, we each contribute. Not because we are the most 'credentialed' but because one sees something no one else can see. Thus, onlyness is an advancement on the idea of talent. Often, talent is defined as those with a specific degree or experience, when onlyness points to inherent capacity. Those can overlap, of course, but if you are the one to enable onlyness in your efforts, through systems and leadership, then you draw on the fuller potential of what exists.

This is the challenge of the day, and one that will unlock the creativity of our firms and our society.

Nilofer Merchant

Nilofer Merchant has personally launched more than 100 products, netting $18B in sales. She's worked for major companies like Apple and Autodesk, and start-ups in the early, early days of the Internet. She is the author of *11 Rules for Creating Value in the #SocialEra* and *The Power of Onlyness* (Viking, 2017). She won the Thinkers50 Future Thinker Award in 2013.

From Erin Meyer

Dear CEO,

Congratulations! You have successfully grown your organization, turning a healthy profit. Now you are looking for international growth opportunities. But before you acquire that company in Malaysia, open an office in Brazil or begin outsourcing to India, be sure to invest time in learning how your corporate culture will interact with the national cultures of the countries you could move into.

Consider the experience of one Silicon Valley high-tech start-up.... let's call it Catchall.

After years of success in the United States, Catchall began international expansion. The corporate culture was anchored in two very strong values: (1) a belief that strong debate and open disagreement are the foundation of good decision-making, and (2) the opinion that hierarchy and deference to authority lead to mistakes and complacency. Catchall hired and trained employees based on these two beliefs, looking for staff who would thrive in a confrontational egalitarian environment. When the company grew internationally, these values went with it. Catchall believed its strong corporate culture to be a key to its notable success.

But its first international acquisition, a company in Stockholm, proved so challenging the subsidiary eventually had to be closed. One Swedish manager explained, 'In Swedish culture, we put such a strong value on consensus building that we avoid disagreeing openly with others. Instead we express differences in opinion gently, so that consensus can gradually emerge. When we were purchased by Catchall, many Swedes felt the confrontational behaviour of their Catchall colleagues was completely inappropriate and maladaptive.' In just six months, Catchall was struggling with startlingly high turnover, and as the company developed a reputation as an aggressive workplace, it became nearly impossible to attract necessary talent.

For its next move, Catchall took a different approach, using a system that I call Culture Mapping to better understand their own organizational culture and compare that to the culture of the next target country.

The Culture Mapping process, which I developed at INSEAD by building on the work of many in my field, is made up of eight scales that represent common management behaviours: Communicating, Evaluating, Leading, Deciding, Trusting, Disagreeing, Scheduling and Persuading. By comparing the relative position of your corporate culture to the cultures where your company plans to expand, you can pinpoint potential areas of conflict and strategize how to deal with them.

Catchall began its next move by mapping out its corporate culture on the eight Culture Map scales, identifying where it stood on each dimension and also which scales seemed most important to the success of the company. The Catchall Culture Map looked something like this (Exhibit A); in particular note dimensions 3 and 6.

Exhibit A

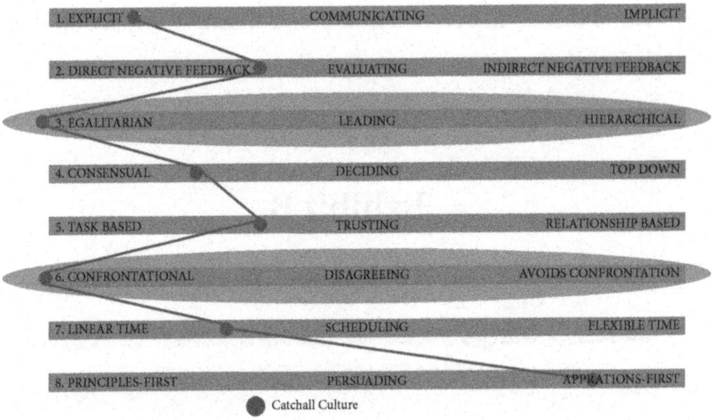

This mapping process allowed Catchall executives to prepare themselves for the ways their corporate culture was likely at odds with the local way of doing things. After a cultural analysis, a company might decide not to move into a particular country after all. Or they could decide some features of their preferred corporate culture might not actually be so essential; they could make some adjustments if a business opportunity looked too promising to pass up.

Comparing Catchall's corporate culture to Swedish national culture, Catchall executives realized that they could have been more aware of how their own company values would clash with the Swedish style, and set a plan in advance to mitigate the difficulty. Exhibit B below shows the two most important dimensions of Catchall corporate culture (3 and 6). Sweden is close to Catchall's corporate culture when it comes to egalitarian behaviour (# 3) but far away on the expression of disagreement (# 6). With some early analysis, they realized they could have addressed this clash before it had such a negative impact on their Swedish initiative.

Exhibit B

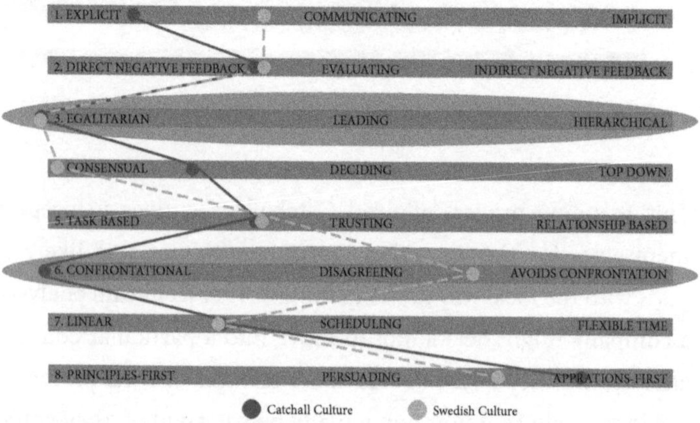

When an opportunity came up in Israel, they realized the Israeli culture's comfort with open disagreement and egalitarian tendency was a perfect match for Catchall's corporate style (see dimensions #3 and #6, Exhibit C).

Exhibit C

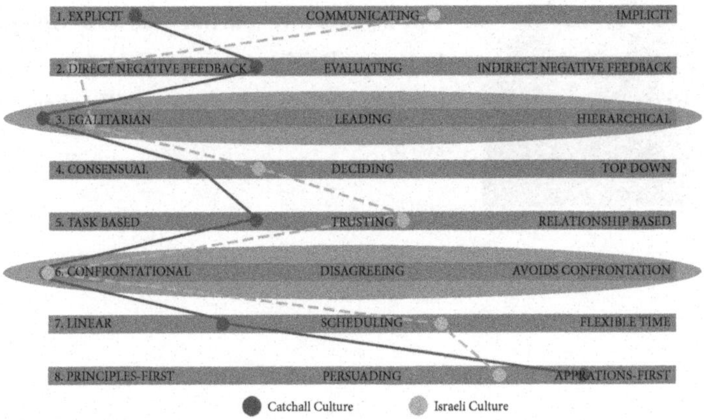

It was apparent from the first negotiations that here employees challenged their bosses in front of others without discomfort from any party, just as was common in the Catchall organizational culture. Catchall proceeded with the deal leading to years of fruitful growth and collaboration.

As your company expands, look carefully at the corporate culture you have fostered at home and pinpoint how that culture will need to adapt to succeed in various local cultures around the world. The Culture Map shows you how.

[signature]

Erin Meyer

A Professor at INSEAD, **Erin Meyer** is author of *The Culture Map: Breaking Through the Invisible Boundaries of Global Business* (Public Affairs, 2014). She won the Future Thinker Award at Thinkers50 2015.

From Lee Newman

Dear CEO,

Your business is not about results, nor is it your role to deliver them. True, your board forcefully demands them, the equity markets await them and your personal wealth banks on them. But your results should not – and logically cannot – be your true mission.

A leader can only lead what can be led, and unfortunately your quarterly numbers fail this basic test. They have a mind of their own. They whisper to the markets when you aren't paying attention. They conspire with your customers behind your back. They are present in every meeting and every conversation, involving every one of your employees, every day of every workweek. They turn a deaf ear to even your most persuasive leadership communications. They are omnipresent, but you cannot lead them.

Distil it all down to first principles, and you'll see that you can lead only two things: Behaviour and Climate. These two should be the focus of all of your efforts. Your mission as CEO should be to invest in understanding the 'what', 'why', 'how' and 'when' of human behaviour, and how behaviour is subtly shaped by the climate within your organization. Nothing more, nothing less. As a leader, if you can positively influence both, great results will follow. Do so poorly, and your results will punish you – as will your board, your markets and your pay cheque. Keep your title of CEO if you want, but your real role should be CBO – the Chief Behaviour Officer – in your organization.

The CBO understands that behaviour drives results

One could spend a lifetime catching up on today's latest thinking about how to lead (most often repackaged versions of yesterday's latest thinking), and doesn't it always come down to numbers? The five keys to effective meetings, the eight steps to leading change, the ten traps of team dynamics. But ultimately, your organization's results are just an infinitely complex aggregation of what happens hourly in every workplace conversation, conflict, team meeting, innovation session, and in the moment-by-moment decisions and actions your employees make, whether they are working alone at their desks, or with others.

So what do you need to know, in a nutshell? Bad behaviours that occur hourly in your workplace are the culprit that kill productivity, reduce engagement, sap motivation and dare I say … hurt your results. Every meeting that goes off-agenda, or need not have been. Every mind that wanders off, while another is still talking. Every disruptive or careless comment, arising from stress or impatience.

Your employees know this, but they desperately need your help to do something about it. I know this too, because I've talked with your employees and studied their 'bad habits' as part of my work at IE's School of Human Sciences and Technology.

I asked them to think of their behaviours as muscles, and to share with me any they think they might train to improve their workplace performance. Of the twenty-two bad habits on my list, your employees on average chose ten or more. So, what are some of the most troublesome bad habits and the per cent of your employees who admit to them? Poor listening (60 per cent), closed-mindedness (50 per cent), impatience working in teams (50 per cent), people talking too much or too little in teams (40 per cent), losing control over emotions (40 per cent) and the list goes on.

In short, your employees are just not 'behaviourally fit', and it costs you. You could blame it on them, except my data shows your employees are identical to those in every organization. It's not *their* problem, it's a *human* problem. We take people, put them in the workplace, ask them to deliver increasingly elevated results, with increasingly reduced budgets – and to balance it all with their lives outside of work (if that's part of their benefit package) – and good behaviours fall by the wayside. Why?

If you accept my proposal to become CBO in your organization, during your training you'll learn that your employees' 'mindware' – what drives their behaviour – is fundamentally limited. Cognitively, attention is like a spotlight that drains a person's batteries; short-term memory is like a whiteboard that has trouble holding information; habitual behaviours are produced by a factory that resists change; and self-control is like a steering wheel that's hard to turn (particularly at the end of a difficult workday). It's no wonder with such limitations that 60–90 per cent of business professionals admit to being poor listeners. And to make matters worse, when your employees experience in-the-moment negative emotions like stress, annoyance, impatience, fear … their already limited mindware works even less well.

So what's to be done?

The CBO knows how to positively shape behaviour

Sir Ken Robinson, a leading thinker on education reform, commented that the real role of leadership should not be command and control, but climate control. And here lies your true mission as the CBO of your organization: to put in place a climate that will innately favour high-quality workplace behaviours, a climate in which your employees can become more behaviourally fit.

You're probably thinking 'financial incentives', but these are a blunt, brute-force tool that too often create exactly the climate that you don't want. No, it's not really about money. Instead, as CBO, you'll have two powerful sets of tools at your disposal.

First, you'll put in place a behavioural fitness training programme for all employees. Not an old-school HR training program, nor a fashionable new programme using the latest buzzwords. Rather, a neuroscience-based method that will help your people hack bad habits to replace them with more productive ones. In the same way that people help each other get in physical shape using tools like Nike+, you'll turn your organization into a fun behaviour-gym where individuals and teams train together to reach new levels of performance. I worked with a bank CEO who asked his management team what behavioural muscle he should train – in this case, it was not listening carefully to their ideas. He put a bright sticker on his phone and in every meeting room to remind him to hack his habit. He also put a money jar on every meeting table. Every time he was caught not listening carefully, he put money in the jar that his team would use for Friday happy hour. CBOs replace dry, standard training programmes that rarely work, with behavioural programmes that do.

Second, you'll lead the design of a workplace climate that favours good behaviours at the expense of bad ones. It's called 'behavioral nudging' and it's grounded in hard science. These will be small, subtle changes in workplace conditions that will have a profound impact on how your employees think and feel, and what they say and do in the moments that populate every workday. For example, you'll work with front-line managers on the way they communicate and the language they use in meetings; you'll nudge problem-solving sessions so that employees argue based on facts rather than on personal positions; you'll create a system for strengths-based development; you'll put in place mobile apps that nudge people to give each other more regular positive feedback; and you'll rethink the design of workspaces to foster behavioural Key Performance Indicators like innovative thinking, collaboration and open-minded debate.

In closing, I urge you to be strong and to let those vexing results go, if only in the amount of time you spend thinking about them. Your board and your shareholders will never know, but when bonus time arrives they will surely thank you and ask how you do it … to which you'll reply, 'good behaviour, and a favourable climate'.

Best to you and your people,

Lee Newman

Lee Newman is dean of IE's School of Human Sciences and Technology, and Professor of Behavior, Leadership & Analytics. He holds a PhD in Cognitive Psychology and in Computer Science, and formerly served as an engagement manager at McKinsey & Co and as a founder and senior manager in technology ventures. He was shortlisted for the Thinkers50 Breakthrough Idea Award in 2015.

From Alex Osterwalder and Yves Pigneur

Dear CEO,

A recent McKinsey study (McKinsey Global Innovation Survey) shows that 80 per cent of your CEO peers think that their current business model is at risk. The research also shows that a mere 6 per cent of your executives are satisfied with the innovation process in your organization.

You have been excellent at executing and improving your proven and successful business models. But as the research above shows, you have not yet found the answer to inventing entirely new business models, value propositions and growth engines.

In fact, managing the present is taking oxygen away from inventing the future. To prevent this from happening, you need a powerful Chief Entrepreneur to focus on the future while you focus on the present. You need to give these entrepreneurs prestige and power and a space for new ideas to flourish and thrive. And you need to change the way your organization is structured so it can systematically churn out new growth engines. Anything less than this is innovation theatre, and that's just not enough.

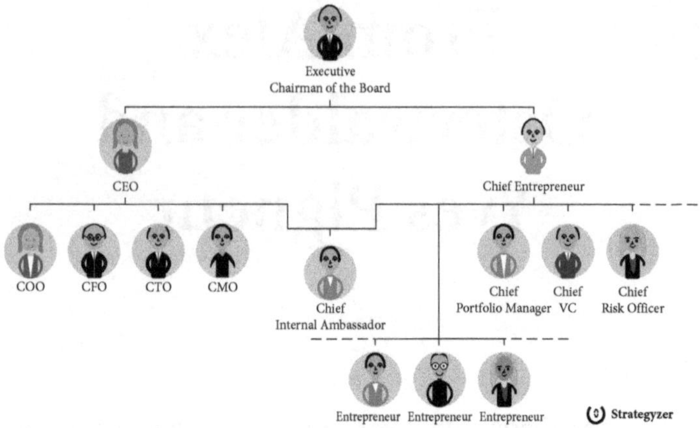

The leadership challenge: Simultaneously manage the present and invent the future

You're likely to be in your current position because you are world class at managing and growing the company's known business model. However, it's no longer enough to 'only' be world class at execution. We like to say that business models and value propositions expire like a yoghurt in the fridge. The reality is that business models are expiring faster than ever before. The likelihood of a CEO managing a single business model through his or her tenure no longer exists. You have to also invent the future, which will require systematically and continuously inventing new business models. You not only have to be world class at executing and improving your current business model, but you also have to be world class at searching and inventing new business models for the future.

That's the real leadership challenge.

Innovation today is about exploiting market opportunities with new business models and value propositions. This does not mean pumping more money into R&D. Product and technology innovation – classic R&D – is not enough to keep you relevant. We can point to businesses like Kodak, Nokia and Blackberry as warning signs of innovative technology companies that went bust. Instead, you have to allocate a percentage of your R&D budget to the exploration of business models and value propositions.

You would have to be schizophrenic, and have more than twenty-four hours in the day, to be world class at both jobs. In order to excel at both, you need a powerful person skilled at execution who focuses on the present, and a powerful person skilled at entrepreneurship who focuses on inventing the future. You need to create an innovation engine that will function alongside your current business. This is a whole new organizational chart of people and skills led at the top by a Chief Entrepreneur.

This 'ambidextrous culture' is how you will survive in the twenty-first century.

What does an innovation engine do?

Your innovation engine is a home for the entrepreneurs inside your business. It's where new growth engines are manufactured and it's managed by a Chief Entrepreneur. It's a space where new business ideas can flourish and thrive. It's a space for new ideas that are very different, or potentially in conflict, from the established business model.

Your innovation engine is not a space where you write business plans for new ideas. Your main goal is to decrease the risk and uncertainty around new ideas. It's a space where you prototype and test new business models and value propositions, where you experiment and gather evidence as cheaply and quickly as possible by getting out the building with methodologies like Lean Startup and Customer Discovery.

It's a myth that innovation is extremely risky and costly – in fact, innovation is only an expensive gamble when you do it wrong. Today the knowledge, tools and processes exist to systematically reduce the market risk inherent to new ideas, business models and value propositions.

The use of visual and practical tools like the Business Model and Value Proposition Canvas will help you shape, prototype and test new business ideas systematically – similar to how architects design new buildings. These tools encourage teams to design quick and rough prototypes that can be tested on customers immediately for fast feedback and learning.

The challenge has changed, and so the organization needs to change

The challenge is that companies need to constantly churn out new business models. Not just new business ideas – but entirely new growth engines year over year. This is a crucial turning point for twenty-first-century organizations, and it requires a new organizational model to address the challenge of constantly churning out new growth engines.

Do you have the organizational structures in place to be world class at executing, but also at churning out new growth engines? On the one hand, your execution engine will need to be world class at managing factories and tolerating zero failure; on the other hand, your innovation engine will need to be world class at experimenting, failing and learning to shape new ideas.

Lastly, your innovation engine will need help from your execution engine – we cannot stress this enough. You need to give entrepreneurs the advantages of a large company. You have to give them access to existing brand credibility, existing customers, existing resources and assets that can be powerful for the innovation engine's exploration of new growth engines. This is what distinguishes internal ventures from start-ups.

Very few companies are good at this ambidextrous culture, but this is changing. Companies are slowly and steadily acting in the face of business model disruption. This is going to be a difficult journey, but you are not alone in this challenge. The truth is, there's never going to be a right time to start. If you don't want to end up like Kodak, Nokia, or Blackberry, then you have to start now.

Sincerely,

Alexander Osterwalder and Yves Pigneur

Winners of the 2015 Thinkers50 Strategy Award, **Alex Osterwalder** and **Yves Pigneur** are authors of the international bestseller *Business Model Generation: A Handbook for Visionaries, Gamechangers and Challengers* (Wiley, 2010).

Osterwalder and Pigneur have followed up with a string of other books, including *Value Proposition Design: How to Create Products and Services Customers Want* and *Business Model You: A One-Page Model for Reinventing Your Career*. They are Thinkers50 ranked thinkers.

From Tom Peters

Dear CEO,

The easy way to write this letter is to use words like 'disruption' in pretty much every paragraph. Then throw in 'big data' and IoT (Internet of Things) as often as possible as well. Indeed, we are bombarded by disruptive forces, and the likes of the IoT and advanced Artificial Intelligence could throw us off stride – or off the bus. (Oh, and 'leadership', 'vision' and 'authenticity' must make at least cameo appearances, too.)

For starters, I urge you to hire the brightest young women (and a few young men) to help you deal with all this madness – as to the 'young' bit, I assume you are wise enough to have two or three 'under thirtys' on your board and even more on your executive team, right? (If not, are you sleeping?)

My friend, the late George Whalin, wrote a superb book titled *Retail Superstars: The 25 Best Independent Stores in America*. I suppose I've given close to 100 copies away – to business owners, division general managers and even accounting and HR leaders. Why? Two reasons. First, it includes between its covers twenty-five acts of unbridled imagination – these frisky independents took on the 'big box' crowd and left them gasping in the dust. Consider Jungle Jim's International Market in Fairfield, Ohio. Customers come from near, far and *very* far to experience its 'shoppertainment' – e.g. 1,600 cheeses, 1,400 hot sauces, 12,000 wines from $8 to $8,000 per bottle. And, hey, Jungle Jim's won a national award for 'Best Restroom in America'. Hard to beat. The second reason I give George's book away is the presence of a single sentence: 'Be the best. It's the only market that's not crowded.' Call it juvenile, if you wish; I choose to label it 'profound'.

Let's move from best restroom to most dog biscuits – two million dog biscuits, to be precise. That's the number that Commerce Bank gave away a few years ago in its determined effort to get customers away from the ATMs (and the competition) and into its branches. I admit to a love affair with founder Vernon Hill's philosophy: 'Are you going to cost cut your way to prosperity? Or are you going to spend your way to prosperity?' '*Over*-invest in our people, *over*-invest in our facilities'. 'Cost cutting is a death spiral. Our whole story is growing revenue'. (FYI, the Germans have played this game to the hilt. Their peerless export record is directly built on the backs of their 'be the best' Mittelstand/mid-size sector.)

The contrarian theory seems to have paid off. In 2007, Hill sold Commerce Bank to TD Bank for $8.5 billion. Then off he and his spunky 'WOW Bank' crew went to the staid UK, opened Metro Bank and again WOWed his way to stunning success. (Full disclosure: In a couple of weeks as I write, I will attend Metro Bank's annual 'Amaze' awards banquet in London.)

I have recently finished a draft of my next and likely last book: *The Excellence Dividend: Meeting the Tech Tide with Work That Wows and Jobs That Last*. It is intended to be a summation of what I've learned in fifty years of managing and observing managers. The toughest part of the process of book writing is picking an epigraph, in this instance a couple of sentences that attempt to capture the spirit of a half century of struggle. I'm pleased with the result, from the mouth of the inimitable Richard Branson, 'Business has to give people enriching, rewarding lives – or it's simply not worth doing'.

It's 'the people' who do the work. It's 'the people' who generate the growth and profit. It's 'the people' that matter.

Damn it.

Okay, I'll stoop this one time to the use of the word 'disruption'. I think that most of our white-collar jobs, including the highest paid, are at risk from AI in particular in the course of the next twenty years. (An Oxford study pegged the at-risk share at 50 per cent.) And I insist that sets up a crystal-clear *moral* obligation for business leaders. As I put it in the new book, 'Your principal moral obligation as a leader is to develop the skillset, "soft" and "hard", of every one of the people in your charge (temporary as well as semi-permanent – there is no such thing, circa 2017, as "permanent") to the maximum extent of your abilities. The bonus: This is also the #1 mid- to long-term profit maximization strategy!' (In his book *Good Business,* Mihaly Csikszentmihalyi says it's business which employs the majority of us, and that said business, therefore, has the civic responsibility to 'increase the sum total of human well-being'. Talk about an aspiration – and challenge.

I had an out-and-out tiff at a recent speech. It was to a group of company franchisees who were complaining bitterly that the intense competitive situation (competitors, technology, regulations) forced them to pay low wages, which in turn often led to outbreaks of shabby work. I acknowledge that I went a little off the rails, chastising them – in the spirit of George Whalin, Vernon

Hill and Richard Branson. I said I thought their avowed goal should be to pay the *highest* wages in the industry – and to enable that by providing a 'be the best service' that would allow them to charge a significantly above-market price. There was substantial pushback – though the (my) day was saved when perhaps their most successful, and quite large, franchisee rose (literally) to my defence and insisted that what I'd said was 'dead on'.

You now pretty much have my mandate – if you relentlessly focus on the excellence of the product or service and the excellence of the staff that designs it, delivers it and constantly re-imagines it, on the whole good things are likely to follow.

I'll leave the final words to Napoleon: 'The art of war does not require complicated maneuvers; the simplest are the best and common sense is fundamental. From which one might wonder how it is generals make blunders; it is because they try to be clever.'

Best wishes, best of luck and remember, be the best – it's the only market that's not crowded.

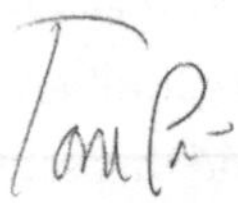

Tom Peters

Tom Peters (tompeters.com) is the co-author of the original business blockbuster *In Search of Excellence*. His other books include the era-defining *Liberation Management* (Macmillan, 1992). He is a member of the Thinkers50 Hall of Fame.

From Gianpiero Petriglieri

Dear CEO,

I have been asked to write you a letter. I am honoured to oblige. I imagine this will find you busy, and perhaps weary, too. Your influence stretches farther than it ever has, reaching beyond the fate of your corporation. And yet, the trust most people have in you, the people on whose behalf you work, is at historical lows. You are both ubiquitous and unreachable, more often admired or reviled than encountered. Therefore, when we address you, let us face it, we often resort to veiled flattery or critiques. Meant to expose your brilliant vision or ill intent. Neither is my aim here. I'd rather like to get to know you better and help out. So I thought I'd ask four questions instead.

Excuse the long preamble. I know. They have often told me to keep it simple and get to the point, for business leaders are short of patience, attention and nuance. I think that is a problem, you see, and also rather insulting. Hence not to indulge that belittling stereotype, I have taken my time. As partial atonement, I'll make this letter a list. Just don't call it a memo, OK?

1. *How do you know that you are leading, and leading well?* Just because you occupy the apex or hub of your company's formal authority structure – whatever polyhedron you use to represent it visually these days that pyramids are out of fashion

– and the word 'leader' is used reflexively to refer to you (a confusing literary convention if you ask me), it does not mean that you are actually leading. How do you know if and when you are? Please, do not point me to your company's annual report or share price. Even if those figures could be directly and unequivocally attributed to your work, which is unlikely, is that all leading means to you? Getting things done? Surely there is more to it. Not only you influence what gets done, but most important, why and how it gets done. Amid the pressures and constituencies that constrain your work, what is the purpose that you orient yourself and others towards? Who benefits from it? What is one thing you cannot measure that you have helped start, change or preserve?

2. *How do you know that you are right?* Assuming your company endorses meritocracy, you are likely to be where you are because you have worked hard, made sound decisions and accurate predictions in the past. Your track record and position, however, make it likely that you are now surrounded by people who vocally agree with you, admire you, maybe even fear you – and most of all expect that you portray some confidence in your vision for the future. All that can distort judgement. How do you know that your convictions and plans rest on a solid ground of current data and are not scaffolded by habit, overconfidence, adulation or blind faith?

3. *Who helps you doubt well?* You are often reminded, and tell others in turn, that as a leader you need to be both self-confident and self-aware. That is much easier said than done. Confidence, the genuine kind, requires a degree of conviction. Self-awareness, on the other hand, is borne out of doubt and

uncomfortable questions. Too much of one can destroy the other; that is why we need help to navigate the tricky waters between the Scylla of numb rigidity and the Charybdis of paralyzing doubt. Left alone at the top, most leaders eventually fall prey to one or the other. Who cares enough to keep you open to alternative views and steady in the face of diversions? Who helps you tell an emerging threat or opportunity from yet another distraction?

4. *What questions do you ask yourself? And others?* Far more important than these questions of mine are the questions *you* ask. The ones you ask yourself and the ones you share with others. Are they similar or different ones, and if they are different, why? Do you invite others to help you predict and shape the future, or do you see it as your job to do it on their behalf? Questions, like facts and goals, have origins and consequences. Do you ever wonder where yours come from, and would you share it?

Your questions matter most because they reveal, sustain and orient your curiosity. Convictions may make you inspiring. Curiosity keeps you alive. If all we get is your well-curated image, directions and results we are bound to remain distant. It is sharing in questions, puzzles, dilemmas and doubts that makes us fellow humans.

Gianpiero Petriglieri

Gianpiero Petriglieri is an associate professor of Organizational Behaviour at INSEAD, where he directs the Management Acceleration Programme for emerging leaders. He was shortlisted for the 2015 Thinkers50 Leadership Award. An earlier version of this article appeared on www.wsj.com on 25 November 2013.

From Doug Ready

Dear CEO,

Not too many of us have the chance to become a CEO. Many rise to senior management roles but far fewer are chosen to lead their organizations as chief executives. As such, perhaps the biggest challenge facing CEOs today is how to not squander the privilege. That's right – leading is an extraordinary privilege – not a burden. If you've been chosen to lead you know have a choice – you can have powerful and lasting impact on thousands of people's lives or you can waste the opportunity. It's as simple as that – you have the choice.

No doubt, there are many forces at play that might tempt you to take the squandered-privilege path. Analysts are hounding you to make the tough calls on employees (who have helped build your business). Lobbyists are pressing you to devise perfectly worded arguments for their cause (against the decency argument you feel in your bones). Investors have a variety of options (if you don't deliver the returns they expect). And if you don't make the calls that are often expected of you, there are plenty of aspiring CEOs among your own top executive team (who are ready to step in if you hesitate to do so). What I'm alarmed about even more is the perverse dynamic that has enabled CEOs to be anointed celebrity status for squeezing 'head count' to the point where employees are feeling more stressed at work than ever before. Moreover, in these environments, resources for training and employee development are viewed as highly discretionary and are therefore subject to relentless budget cutting. In low-growth environments, it's perceived as easier and more cost-effective to replace employees rather than investing in them.

With these and other pressures on your plate, why bother thinking about your role on a higher level – just execute, deliver results and the rest will take care of itself – right? So let me return to my initial argument – you have choices. As such, my question for you is: ***What will your legacy be as CEO?*** The question is not what do I hope it will be or what could it be in a different environment, but what will it be, as you have the choice.

Let me try to answer my own question to see if it reflects how you feel. I would hope that you would love to lead an organization where employees said they felt *proud*, *excited* and yet *humbled* to work there. *Proud* because your organization is guided by a compelling sense of purpose, and you have challenged employees to live up to that purpose every day. *Excited* because you have created a work environment in which people feel challenged and stretched, providing them with opportunities to grow, contribute to building your business, and at the same time, develop to their fullest potential. And *humbled*, because employees know that your decisions, those of your leaders, and ultimately their decisions are rooted in and guided by a well-understood set of core values and guiding principles.

This environment, of course, would not be limited to your employees. The communities in which you operate would feel proud that you call their community home – because it feels that way. What's more, your business partners and customers would feel that doing business with you is the equivalent of the time-honoured handshake. Now that's an enviable legacy indeed. You've built and led an organization that is purpose-driven, performance-oriented and principles-led. Your people are proud to call your company home, excited to help you build it and feel a deep sense of humility that they are able to derive meaning from their work. It doesn't get any better than that!

Doug Ready

Doug Ready is the founder and CEO of the International Consortium for Executive Development Research (ICEDR) and a senior lecturer at MIT's Sloan School of Management. Prior to joining MIT, Ready was a dean and faculty member at Boston University, Babson College, Kenan-Flagler Business School and London Business School. He is a Thinkers50 ranked thinker.

From Alf Rehn

No, 'Innovation' Won't Save You. But Wicked Problems Might

Dear CEO,

Dear friend, as I write to you on this day of yet another disappointing innovation reveal, let me tell you that I know how you feel. I know, and I feel for you. It's not really your fault. You did exactly as they told you to. You listened to the gurus, you read the books, you went to the conferences and you did your best to follow their advice. And what advice was that? Well, in short, that you need to change, swiftly. They said you needed to 'innovate or die', to look for new opportunities, to adapt to the new technological trends. They said you need to create 'an innovative organization', one that embraced creativity and thought outside the box (that vile, stupid cliché). They said you need to disrupt yourself before you got disrupted, become future-oriented rather than hidebound, listen to customers and the group genius of your organization and turn from traditionalism towards trendspotting. You got it, because you're smart like that, and you tried. Oh, how you tried.

The problem, however, was that things didn't go quite as smoothly as advertised. You tried to support innovation and creativity in your organization, yet precious little changed. You hired consultants with funky eyeglasses and a winning way with Post-It® notes, but when they left, things went back to normal quick as can be. You invested money in innovation projects, but surprisingly few of these resulted in much of anything, although you'd rather die than confess that to the media. In fact, although you can never say it out loud, you have your doubts about how innovative your new products really are. Sure, you say they're huge steps forward, and you talk about your new app and how you're all about digitalization, but in the long dark hours of the night you think about whether it's all it is cracked up to be. I know it's scary, and I'm here to tell you it's OK. You did nothing wrong. You were misled.

Innovation was supposed to change the world, but often ended up delivering cheap trinkets, radical in name only. Innovation was supposed to revolutionize your company, but ended up giving you more of the same. Innovation was supposed to be everything traditional management is not, but ended up co-opted by consultants, perverted by pundits and mangled by managers. So no, innovation, or more to the point, 'innovation', won't save you. In fact, your false faith in it might bring about your doom. The last thing you need is to invest good money in bad hype, or fatigue your already bedraggled organization with another shiny-happy innovation initiative that rewards consultants and sizzle over competence and steak.

At the same time, there is a way forward, even if it doesn't look anything like a calm, blue ocean. The reason 'innovation' so often fails to live up to the grandiose words ascribed to it – 'radical', 'revolutionary', 'disruptive' – can in part be tracked down to the manner in which we lost that great ambition that was supposed to drive innovation. We wanted flying cars and to change the world, and we got 140 characters about sugared water, to conflate the sayings of Peter Thiel and Steve Jobs.

As innovation, as a word, became used for everything from any gadget sold to an increasingly blasé group of affluent consumers to the latest variation of ready-made soups, it began losing more and more of its meaning. Today, the people in your organization are neither energized by nor interested in innovation, as it means everything and anything. If you think about it, and I know you do, they have actually come to despise the word, as to them it represents little more than the manner in which a once proud and powerful word has been co-opted by those who care more about looking good than doing good.

But do not despair. There are still things to do in this world, still meaningful projects to attempt. There are wicked problems in this world – problems of ecology, inequality, grand technological challenges – worthy of your interest in innovation. While the consultants sell you the sugared water of innovation, now with extra disruption, you could marshal the resources of your corporation and make innovation meaningful again. You've never had more tools with which to attack wicked problem, nor more competencies with which to start changing the world.

You see, it was never meant to be all about innovation. Innovation was the tool with which to do great things, not the thing in itself. By focusing on innovation for innovation's sake, you lost track of what really matters – meaningful change, solving big problems, creating a better world. So forget about the pretty words and the fancy conferences. Think instead of what is possible beyond innovation, when we care less about what makes for good PR and more about what builds a better world. Think about what you can achieve when you care more about ambitious ideas than whether you look 'innovative' or not. Think about what happens when an organization is energized by meaningful issues, rather than fatigued by me-too thinking.

Wickedly yours,

Alf Rehn

Alf Rehn (alfrehn.com) is a Finnish academic, speaker and author of *Dangerous Ideas* (Marshall Cavendish, 2011) and co-author of *Trendspotting* (ebook, 2013). He was shortlisted for the Thinkers50 Innovation Award in 2015.

From Jonas Ridderstråle and Kjell Nordstrom

Dear CEO,

Witness the rise of aggressively independent and technologically savvy women – from the fictional likes of Lisbeth Salander from *The Girl with the Dragon Tattoo*, to the factual ones of Germany's Angela Merkel and the United Kingdom's Theresa May. This is the Gaga Saga – the tale of modern life on our planet. A more than a century-long struggle for basic human rights has now become a self-propelling and self-reinforcing process. There ain't no stopping *them* now.

Women are being liberated by the new, open era. Women are the great unsung power in our societies, on our workforces and in our organizations. Women now hold more wealth than ever in history and work for pay in unparalleled numbers. So, you and your company better get ready for the world of womenomics!

Here's why. And it has little to do with equality or fairness. That matters too, but for the time being let's focus on the facts. The conditions have changed. Historically, most women spent 80 per cent of their lives giving birth to and taking care of their kids. They had 20 per cent that they could devote to other things. Today, even in the developing world where we've seen a dramatic shift over the last thirty years, we live longer lives and infant mortality rates are down. This means that women simultaneously are less time-constrained and have fewer childbirths to worry about. Indeed, when economies grow, one of the first effects is decreasing birth rates.

Economic development and the liberation of women from the traditional subservient role tend to go hand in hand. Capitalism and feminism may be odd bedfellows, but bedfellows nevertheless. Even in the most conservative bastions of male chauvinism, young women now have more time on their hands. From 80/20 to 20/80.

And what do many of these women use that extra time for? When we ask executive crowds this question, half the times a guy will burst out: shopping! And while that may very well be true – after all, we've been told that these days men dominate only three domestic purchasing decisions, those regarding the purchase of a lawnmower, grill or chainsaw – the right answer is: studying. If you, like us, spend a lot of time at university campuses around the world – from the Americas to Europe, in Asia and beyond, this is so obvious. Young women study to an extent that we've never, ever witnessed before. We can see it in the statistics. We know what young women around the world are up to. What the young men are doing we don't know! ESPN and Sky Sports, drinking beer and playing World of Warcraft – no idea, but they are no longer the dominant force in our educational system.

This development holds tremendous implications for our societies, for your company and indeed for you. Firstly, in a world where wealth is created with wisdom, we are all players in a great global attraction game for talent. Most Western companies already suffer from a shortage of competence, and if they don't they most certainly will in a few years as competition intensifies and also the late baby-boomers move into retirement. In five to ten years they will have to go fish in a talent gene pool that is dramatically different from one of the past. And the stark truth is that most corporations are still built by men, for men, to sell stuff to men.

This leads us to our second and final point. Increasingly, your key customers will be female, and it does not matter if you are in B2B or B2C (unless you sell lawnmowers, grills and chain-saws, that is). Unfortunately, most executives still treat women as if they were just small men! They are not. Men and women are different. Ignore those differences at your peril. Exploit them and you'll realize that there are riches awaiting you in 'Girlville'.

Still not convinced? Consider this. One of dimensions in which men and women differ is in how we relate to risk. Women, on average, take less risk than men. Sometimes, you want a lot of risk-taking and other times you want less. Let's assume that tomorrow you are undergoing open heart surgery. Here's the question: Do you want a surgeon who takes a lot of risk or a little? The answer is, of course, obvious. Few of us would opt for the one who strolls in and explains that today the surgical team is going to wing it. Now, think about business. With this as a backdrop, the two of us have a little hypothesis. What if Lehman Brothers had instead been managed by the Lehman Sisters? Do you think we could have avoided many of the issues that some of us are still struggling with?

Sincerely,

Joan and Kelly (f.k.a. Jonas and Kjell)

Jonas Ridderstråle and **Kjell Nordstrom** are authors of the international bestsellers *Funky Business* and *Karaoke Capitalism* (FT/Prentice Hall, 2004).

They have been included in the Thinkers50 on six occasions. Ridderstråle is also author (with Julian Birkinshaw) of *Fast/Forward* (Stanford Business Books, 2017).

From Antonio Nieto-Rodriguez

Dear CEO,

I believe CEOs are facing the most challenging era in management history, far beyond the Great Depression. The past decade has seen fierce competition arising due to highest levels of globalization, combined with geological instability in a sluggish economy, aggravated by a lack of engagement by a growing size of the workforce, and an unprecedented pressure to deliver short-term results.

To become better equipped for competing and surviving in this new era, organizations have moved into a reactive mode, investing and launching a vast amount of projects: from acquisitions, to digitalization, to new products, going through several reorganizations, ruthless cost reductions up to the breakup of long-standing businesses into several smaller ones.

The reality is that organizations are struggling to reap the benefits of all these projects, but not only that, they have become highly unfocused. Senior executives that lack a shared vision and are not aligned on the top priorities, end up working in silos. All this has a devastating effect on the culture and the capacity of implementing the organization's strategy.

The massive increase in projects introduced by organizations in the past decade has created confusion among managers and employees. In addition, thanks to this leap-forward strategy, many businesses have moved away from their 'core', spreading their resources too thinly, making it very hard to understand where the organization is going.

The number of priorities has also increased. Being customer centric or innovative is not enough. Organizations have to be that, but also efficient, entrepreneurial, intrapreneurial, mindful, compliant, nimble, lean and much more. Every new priority added to the existing ones increases the complexity of the organization and the environment managers have to operate and lead their teams. At the same time, employees have reached a state of 'change-fatigue', tired and demotivated from non-stop changes in their organizations, not knowing whether they have to work on the day-to-day activities or to spend their time in long-term projects.

This current state of play makes it tough for manager to see through the clutter and understand the most important activities to focus their time and effort on. This hampers the ability of organizations to execute their strategies successfully and keep their employees engaged and motivated.

Today CEOs have much less time to act than a decade ago. Markets, shareholders and even their executive teams have become less patient; they look for clarity of direction with immediate results. Yet, many are still dragging along, unable to take the tough decisions.

If value creation, or at worst, value preservation, is the number one responsibility of any CEO and board of directors, they have to take immediate action now. The longer it takes you to make the difficult choices, to prioritize your priorities, to stop projects and products that are far from your core … the more chances you have to destroy value and risk going out of the market.

The following seven questions will help you determine how big the gap is:

1. What is your organization's purpose and is it the same for all the organizations?
2. Are our priorities clear and aligned to your purpose?
3. Can you list your top ten strategic projects?
4. Do you regularly cancel projects?
5. Is your executive team a group of individuals or a 'real team', fully on-board and 100 per cent engaged in delivering your organization's purpose and vision?
6. Do you have the right people to deliver your purpose? Are they working where they are at their best?
7. How do you know if you are on track implementing your strategy?

In response to all of these issues and questions, I propose a Project Revolution. This is composed of three simple concepts, proven successful in other organizations, such as Lego, Western Union and Microsoft. They are easily understood, and have a profound impact on your organization's culture and ways of working. They do, however, require the CEO's sponsorship and full involvement following through till completion. The engagement of the entire executive team, cascaded through the organization, is also required. If seriously taken, you will experience significant improvements in nine to twelve months.

Implement the 'Hierarchy of Purpose'

- Purpose: is the alma mater of your organization that the strategic vision should support.
- Priorities: what matters most to the organization now and in the future.
- Projects: invest in projects that align with the purpose, vision and priorities; stop up to 50 per cent of the rest.
- People: choose the best people to execute on those projects.
- Performance: identify precise targets that will measure real progress.

Adopt the 'Projects Manifesto'

- Think projects when delivering and growing your business.
- Increase your projects' capabilities to drive execution.
- Create project teams instead of working in groups.
- Sell project instead of products or services.
- CEOs are the ultimate project managers.
- Break through silos through projects.

Become a 'Focused Organization'

Focused organizations have a culture of getting the right things done, achieving their strategic goals, having high-performing teams and working with fully engaged employees. Their hierarchy of purpose is very narrow, often based on one or two priorities well known to all the individuals in the organization. They apply the 'Less Is More' principle: less priorities, less projects, more benefits, more results.

Working on the previous two concepts will help you become a Focused Organization and join Apple, Ryan Air, Amazon and many more.

Antonio Nieto-Rodriguez

Antonio Nieto-Rodriguez (antonionietorodriguez.com) is Director of the Program Management Office at GlaxoSmithKline Vaccines and Chair of the Project Management Institute. He is author of the *The Focused Organization* (Routledge, 2012). He was included in the Thinkers50 Radar for 2017.

From Deborah Rowland

Dear Mr/Mrs/Miss/Ms CEO,

I can imagine what it must be like to be in your shoes right now, facing the most pressing leadership challenge of our era: *how to lead ongoing change in an age of disruption and uncertainty*. Do you ever find yourself pondering about how to build the capacity of your organization to operate in this now-required state of continual adaptation?

Just take a look around us at the current state of play. Digital technological innovation, in particular, and the associated rise of social media platforms have been just one unquestionable market disrupter. Who is the 'Uber-equivalent competitor', for you? In this increasingly unpredictable and interconnected world, in which lateral peer-to-peer networks appear as stronger influencing mechanism on change than the traditional, formal, vertical hierarchy, the average time a company stays on the Standard & Poor index is now just seventeen years, down from seventy-five in the middle of the last century. If you don't continually innovate, you could be out.

Why can't we go on leading our companies as we have? Why do we need to change how we change – and now? Okay, the pace of change is accelerating, its complexity and systemic nature now make it hard to unilaterally control, and our traditional organizational structures are just plainly unfit for twenty-first-century agility, but I sense, above all else, that people are increasingly fed up with how the world is being run. We see that in the rise of 'populism' and its backlash against the political and corporate elite who, in the still post–economic crisis austerity world, are frequently deemed to be just feathering their own nest. If CEOs lose the trust of society, what is your mandate to lead? The era in which big leaders in traditional institutions could unilaterally dictate to other members of society what was best for them, is over.

What's more, if we don't get a better grip on how we lead ongoing change – acting responsibly, harnessing new technologies and collaborating across borders – our very planet's survival is at stake.

So, what are the biggest questions I believe you need to address? I have two. First and foremost, what is the most successful approach to the implementation of change in today's world – where top-down dictates and planned, predictable linear change programmes no longer cut it? Second, what are the leadership skills that you and your top team need to cultivate in order to build the capacity of your organization to be in a constant state of change?

Addressing the first question, I ask that you attend equally to the *how*, or your process for change, as you do to the *what,* your change solution. Your choice of approach really is fateful. It will determine where you end up. My research suggests that an emergent change approach is most suited to today's world. This approach sets just a loose intention, a few 'hard rules' that guide people's behaviour, but then reduces formal hierarchy and centrally run programmes and instead allows for self-organization and empowered local innovation – particularly at the boundary of your organization where it meets novelty. Emergent change also moves step-by-step in a trial-and-error way. So give up your fixed grand plans. Stay nimble!

And then the question of your – and your team's – change leadership skill. I have found that a skilful combination of 'fierce naming of reality' and the provision of non-anxious, affirming leadership – where difficult conversations are not avoided and people feel safe to take risk – is the number one practice you have to *do*. But it doesn't stop there. My research has shown that this outer practice needs to be anteceded by a certain inner quality of *being* as a leader. When you are mindfully able to notice and regulate your mental and emotional states, you will draw from a deep still well of calmness, resourcefulness and non-ego-led courage that enable you to approach ongoing turbulence and challenging conditions with discernment and poise. Get and give feedback within your top team on these skills.

Leading big change in today's world is not for the faint hearted. It is for the bold and big hearted. Our world is getting increasingly unpredictable, dynamic and interconnected. This makes change endemic, fast paced, systemic and complex. Leading such volatility requires a certain type of leadership, one that not only acts boldly, able to absorb personal risks and attack, but also holds humanity at its core.

Above all else, look after yourself. Find those spaces of stillness to recharge the batteries – even if that is just a 30-minute walk outdoors at lunchtime. I wish you well!

Deborah Rowland

Deborah Rowland (deborahrowland.com) has led change in major global organizations including Shell, Gucci, BBC Worldwide and PepsiCo, where she was Vice President of Organizational & Management Development. Her book *Still Moving* (Wiley, 2017) is based on groundbreaking research into the realities of managing change.

From Juan Pablo Vazquez Sampere

Don't Be a 'COO on Steroids'; Be a CEO Who 'Feels Like the Future'

Dear CEO,

Most CEOs think that keeping the top job is about being 'a COO on steroids'. Granted, many of them got the position because they are great at implementation, but it turns out that increasing margins by selling more units or by increasing efficiency throughout the company won't help you keep the top job.

Consider Amazon and Walmart, both companies which are very well managed. The names of the companies will likely prompt a reaction from you. One feels like future, the other, not so much.

The reality is that employees, investors and stakeholders will back you up if you represent the future. But, if you are simply a great manager, people will have the feeling that you are about discounting the company's future.

So how can you make your company mean and feel like future? The answer is simple to explain but very difficult to implement: if your business is from the pre-Internet era, you have to understand that it is probably built on a set of underlying assumptions that will no longer hold true in a few years. For instance, there is a belief that your cash reserves will keep disruptors at bay, or that your fixed assets (plants, land, etc.) are unique and irreplaceable, or that government regulation will always be on your side, etc.

At this very same moment, someone, somewhere is developing a business model that circumvents one of these underlying assumptions and will threaten your core business, but if you wait for them so show up in your numbers, it will already be too late. The good news is that as a CEO you no longer need to decide solely based on the numbers; you can scan people for feelings and use that as a guide for new net growth.

Consider US Steel. In just a few years, minimills disrupted the entire steel industry by entering the market using electricity to produce steel. Today US Steel is a shadow of what it was. This has nothing to do with incompetence. The problem was that producing steel with electricity was more expensive than using the traditional method. US Steel watched the entire process of how a new technology that was initially more expensive than theirs took over the market. But they looked at this process with the underlying assumption that there was excess capacity. Cost accounting practices teach managers that as long as you have unused production capacity, your cost is lower than new capacity. By sticking to that decision and running the numbers that way, even when minimills had taken over a significant portion of the market, US Steel became a poster child of how not to react to a disruptor.

Do you really want to be that CEO? Do you really want to be remembered that way?

There are other examples where start-ups not only start with a cost disadvantage that minimizes the responses of established firms but also leverage on other assets, such as distribution. Think of Southwest Airlines and Dell. In the case of Southwest, established airlines thought that the hub-and-spoke model was the only one that made sense; Southwest introduced the point-to-point route with a plane that was costlier to operate. Likewise, Dell challenged the underlying assumption that if you control the stores, you can't enter the PC business. By outsourcing production and focusing on leveraging its direct model, Dell significantly challenged the sustainability of HP, IBM, etc. in their PC business.

In conclusion, people can distinguish between a 'COO on steroids' and a 'CEO who feels like the future'. Maybe they can't verbalize the difference, but it is there. This difference is manageable. By understanding the underlying assumptions of your current business model, you can solve the paradox of managing a well-run organization that is delivering on the numbers but that nobody thinks will exist in the future to another organization that people consider is part of the disruptive change.

Juan Pablo Vazquez Sampere

Juan Pablo Vazquez Sampere is a professor at IE Business School and frequent HBR blogger applying disruptive innovation concepts to current managerial challenges. He was shortlisted for the Thinkers50 Innovation award in 2015.

[illegible]

Juan Pablo Vázquez Sampere

[illegible]

From Christian Stadler

Dear CEO,

Have you ever watched a restaurant's kitchen during the lunchtime rush? Pots and pans are flying everywhere while orders pile in and in the midst of the chaos the head chef has to keep her calm.

How does she do it? Working hard and fast, of course, but above all by prioritizing and directing tasks. I bet your job feels somehow similar with multiple demands piling in at the same time. So what should be your priorities?

First, ensure strategic ambidexterity

It's great to talk about exploration, innovation and new ideas but shareholders want to see returns. Exploitation, efficiency and cost-cutting help to achieve that but naturally they are less popular with employees.

To achieve sustainable competitive advantage, you have to do both. As a scholar, I could point you to a highly cited 1991 article by Jim March on this topic (yes, this idea has been around!) but a brief look to giants like Apple or Google would do as well. Both manage to keep unit costs down and remain at the cutting edge of technology. The latter has decided to reorganize its business so that Google Search and YouTube can optimize proven business models, while Google X and Google Capital provide the room to experiment. If you want to make a living today, but be ready for tomorrow, make sure your company is ambidextrous too!

Second, give diversification another shot

In the 1990s and 2000s, the growth path seemed obvious. Concentrate on your core business and take it international. After all, tariffs were coming down and globalization was bringing the world together. Remember the global village?

To some extent, this is still true, but there is also a backlash from those who benefitted less from these developments. The result: borders are real. In a recent study with two colleagues, Michael Mayer and Julia Hautz, I showed that companies without prior international experience lose money (overall, not just internationally) for the first five years of their effort to do business overseas and the Return on Assets is only half of those who stay local in the five years after that.

Instead, why not leverage your resources across industries? Tata, Infosys and Samsung have shown that their ability to share talent, brand, networks and capital puts them ahead of others trying to navigate challenging emerging economies. But slightly broader agendas are becoming visible in Europe and the United States as well. Once again tech giants such as Google come to mind, but efforts by Uber to move into food delivery or Snapchat's flirt with financial services point in a similar direction. If you have resources that can be re-applied elsewhere, ask yourself why not?

Third, Africa will be the next China

Volkswagen first went to China in 1978 and signed a contract to manufacture vehicles in Shanghai in 1984. It held the leading position in this market for over twenty-five years. Africa will play out the same way.

Those who invest now will dominate later. With falling commodity prices, Africa might look less attractive, but the opposite is the case. It's cheaper to enter today than a couple of years ago while demographics tell a clear story: fifty-two cities with more than a million inhabitants and a growing middle class are starting to turn into attractive markets.

There are also exciting technological developments. With 17 million bank accounts and a transaction volume equivalent to 42 per cent of Kenya's GDP in 2015, M-Pesa is the world's most successful mobile payment system. It also created a new ecosystem. M-Kopa sells home solar systems, which people pay through instalments on an integrated mobile payments system using M-Pesa. It provides electricity to 300,000 homes today! So the remaining question is how you can navigate the challenging institutional environment. M-Pesa provides the answer. Vodafone partnered with Kenya's largest telecom operator to launch M-Pesa, so follow its lead. Local partners will provide the links necessary to succeed.

Let me return once again to the kitchen before I end my letter. Some of the best dishes have a few powerful ingredients. Strategy works in a similar manner. Strategic ambidexterity, diversification and an Africa plan are today's ingredients for a three-star company.

Best,

Christian Stadler

Christian Stadler is Professor of Strategic Management at Warwick Business School. Previously, he held positions at the University of Bath School of Management, Tuck School of Business at Dartmouth and Innsbruck University. He is the author of *Enduring Success* (Kogan Page, 2011) and has been selected as part of the Thinkers50 Radar list of thinkers for the future.

From Henry Stewart

Dear CEO,

Let me paint a common scenario. One of your people comes to you and says, 'I love my job. I love the people I work with. I'm even happy with what I'm being paid. But …. I can't stand my manager.'

What generally happens next? Sooner or later, the person leaves. We know that people join companies and, all too often, leave managers.

There is a solution to this. At my company, Happy Ltd, it takes just a few minutes to deal with. We simply ask, 'Who would you like instead?' Yes, this is our simple concept: **Let people choose their managers.**

According to one survey, 48 per cent of the working population would take a pay cut to be able to change their managers. That's how bad things are.

This approach does sometimes need a little adjustment to structures. Companies who adopt this approach go on to separate people management from strategy. Because why do we assume people are going to be good at both?

Each member of staff gets to choose their manager, the person who provides support and challenge, who meets them regularly and coaches them to set their own ambitious targets. A separate person, with no line management connection, may be responsible for strategy for the department.

If this sounds odd, think of projects. In many organizations, people work for weeks or months on a project. And their project manager is often not their line manager. But it works.

The most common response I get, and you may be thinking it, is, 'what happens to those that don't get chosen?' Never mind those who live lives of misery under managers who should not be in that role. Never mind the low productivity from demotivated staff under managers who diminish them. People's key concern is all too often what happens to those people who nobody wants to have as their manager.

What happens to those who don't get chosen? They get to do something else.

We worked with one company which had a brilliant marketing director, who I will call Mary. She was brilliant at marketing, but she was not a great people manager and half her staff left every year. The company came to us to help them solve it. They had to keep her marketing skills but they had to stop that staff turnover; it was costing them a fortune.

The answer was, of course, simple. Mary was moved to a position where she spent all her time doing marketing. We consulted the team and found out who they wanted to be managed by. And we made the switch.

And guess who was happiest at that change? Yes, Mary was over the moon. She got to spend all her time doing what she was great at.

Don't get me wrong. For many people, the managing of people is what they love. It is what gets them up in the morning and what they remember long after they finish a job. But for others, it just isn't – even after lots of training – one of their strengths.

Another example. We worked with a software company called Cougar back in England. At the end of an awayday with all the project managers, several of them came to us and said, 'We don't want to be managers any more. We're going to go back and tell Clive (the MD).'

How did Clive react? He was delighted, he'd been wondering how to tackle the issue. So they put in place a judo belt system, where coders start at yellow and move up all the way to brown and black. You can imagine that the prestige of being a black belt coder is every bit as good, probably better, than being a top manager.

Or take Apple. You will know that Apple was founded by Steve Jobs and Steve Wozniak. But do you know the difficulty Steve Jobs had getting Woz to leave Hewlett Packard to set up Apple? He explained that he would no longer be a small cog, but would manage a whole team of engineers. Woz said no, he reckoned he'd stay at HP. Jobs kept trying to persuade him, emphasizing his importance and how many people he'd be in charge of.

Then Apple investor Mike Markulla took Steve Jobs aside and explained that Woz just wanted to be an engineer. He didn't want to be responsible for other people. Jobs changed his approach: he offered Woz great kit, all the resources he needed and promised, 'Woz, you will never have to manage anybody'. That sounded good to Woz and he made the move. The rest is history.

There will be people in your business who are great engineers, or great salespeople or great accountants, or great strategists, but whose strength is not the people bit. You need a promotion path for them that doesn't involve managing others.

If you take this simple step of letting people choose their manager, it will lead not just to a happier workforce, but probably a more productive workforce and certainly to a lower staff turnover.

Yours

Henry Stewart

Henry Stewart is the author of *The Happiness Manifesto* and Chief Happiness Officer at the London-based IT training company Happy. He has been on the Thinkers50 Radar.

From Kate Sweetman

Dear CEO,

I have someone I'd like you to meet. His name is Tom Shaw, more commonly known as TShaw.

But first, let's discuss your role as a CEO.

You have the most powerful position in the company. But your position is a precarious one. Your success is never within your complete control because the complex dynamics of the competitive, global and disruptive landscape lie outside your jurisdiction.

And you also can't control your people. Sure, you can install Key Performance Indicators. But you and I both know that the rollout of inherently imperfect performance management tools will not generate the unbridled will to succeed throughout the enterprise that you really need, especially when the road ahead is uncertain and threats can come from any direction in today's very challenging Age of Disruption.

You depend heavily upon employee insights, intelligence, intentions and discretionary effort to meet your targets. That's daunting considering how much that means relying on mere human beings who sometimes – maybe often – worry more about their own career, pay cheque, mortgage, children's college tuitions and aging parents than the actual work. In the VUCA (Volatility, Uncertainty, Complexity, Ambiguity) world, the emotional, mental and physical bandwidth of leaders and employees are likely as stretched as yours. Perhaps more.

So, here's a big question: How can you prepare your organization to break old records? To define and achieve new goals far beyond the ordinary? To truly and *gladly* devote their individual talents and energies to the larger purpose of the organization?

One answer comes from my former client Denis Sullivan, a past SVP of Workforce Development and HR for Verizon Wireless. Denis calls it the 'Power of Being and Belonging'. The notion of *Being* means striving to achieve one's personal best in whatever role you are in. *Belonging* means to put team success above individual triumph and recognition.

With that said, meet Tom Shaw. We all know him as TShaw. TShaw is a high school physics teacher in the greater Boston area. He was recently named one of Milton High School's Teacher of the Year and was also recognized as the Coach of the Year in Track and Cross Country for all of Massachusetts. I know TShaw because he coached my girls when they decided to join the track team to keep in shape and ended up, to their own surprise, as part of a ridiculously successful champion team.

TShaw is a master of this Being and Belonging. He uses this powerful combination to great effect: Within two years of becoming Milton's head track coach, his run-of-the-mill girls track team smashed every record at Milton High. They took first in their Division, then in the State, then in the Region. Capping the season: The 8 × 800 relay team went on to Nationals and medaled, creating four all-American athletes. Whew.

No one was more amazed by their performance than the girls themselves. 'He made us better than we ever knew we could be', marvelled one winner. 'Yes, we ran for ourselves. But way more than that, we ran for our teammates so that THEY could win.'

When TShaw shifts the girls' mindsets towards Being (one's personal best) and Belonging (to a tribe of sister athletes), he unleashes individual and collective energy. My observations of the changes he creates in them:

- ***Mindset 1: Team Above Self*** – The shared mindset is: *I want to personally excel beyond anything I have ever accomplished so that my team will win.*
- ***Mindset 2: Coach Individuals, Not Just the Team*** – TShaw helps each girl realize they could be MUCH better than they ever imagined for themselves. He has an almost encyclopedic knowledge of every girl's strength, weakness and potential. He also helps them create a personal game plan for success.
- ***Mindset 3: Leverage Peer Support and Coaching*** – TShaw ensures that everyone knows each other's goals. Before a meet, team members share their goals for that meet one by one in front of their teammates: what they are confident about and what they are afraid of. Their teammates always cheer them on in achieving their dreams and managing their fears.
- ***Mindset 4: Align to Strengths*** – TShaw freely rotates girls to different events after watching them warm up and assessing their headset that day. Girls understood that garnering points for the team might cost them in attaining

individual records, but, to them, this is no sacrifice because the team benefits.

- ***Mindset 5: Everyone Plays and Everyone Contributes*** – Every girl who tries out for the team is accepted, and nobody sits on the bench. The key to excellence is ensuring that everyone has a meaningful role that aligns both best to her talents and passions as well as to the team need.
- ***Mindset 6: Deep Personal Trust Is the Secret Sauce of Hi-Performance Teams*** – The entire team socializes the night before a meet at one of the players' homes. Attendance is mandatory, singing is abundant and the bonding is palpable.

Tapping into this human capital strategy of *Being and Belonging*, and unleashing the inspiration and passion that comes with that, can turn into the ultimate intangible sustainable competitive advantage for an organization. And it all begins with mindsets.

My dear CEO friend, imagine the returns in your organization if every individual and team maximizes their effort like the Milton High School girls track and cross country team. It can happen.

Mark Zuckerberg and Priscilla Chan recently committed 99 per cent of their wealth to the *Chan Zuckerberg Initiative*. Their end goal is to improve education, cure diseases, connect people and build stronger communities around the globe. Priscilla summed up their strategy in this fashion: 'The only way to achieve our full potential is to channel the talents, ideas, and contributions of every person in the world.' It sounds like *Being and Belonging* to me!

Thanks for allowing me to provide thoughts into your most important role.

Kate Sweetman

The founding principal of SweetmanCragun, **Kate Sweetman** has featured on the Thinkers50 Radar and is the co-author with Shane Cragun of *Reinvention* (Greenleaf, 2016).

From Don Tapscott

Embrace the Second Era of the Internet

Dear CIO,

For the last century, academics and business leaders have shaped the practice of modern management. The main theories, tenets and behaviours of managers have worked well overall in building corporations – largely hierarchical, insular and horizontally or vertically integrated.

Until now. The blockchain technology underlying cryptocurrencies such as Bitcoin will effect profound changes in the nature of firms: how they are funded and managed, how they create value and how they perform basic functions like marketing and accounting. In some cases, software will replace management altogether.

The Internet today connects billions of people around the world, and certainly it's great for communicating and collaborating online. But because it's built for moving and storing information, and not *value*, it has done little to change the corporation and the nature of business. When you send information to someone, like an email, Word document or PDF, you're really sending a copy, not the original. It's OK (and indeed advantageous) for people to print a copy of their PowerPoint file, but not OK to print, say, money, stocks, Intellectual property or music. So with the Internet of information we have to rely on powerful intermediaries to establish trust. Banks, governments and even social media companies like Facebook all do the work of establishing our identity and helping us own and transfer assets and settle the transactions.

Overall, they do a pretty good job – but there are limitations. They use centralized servers, which can be hacked. They take a piece of the value for performing this service – say 10 per cent to send some money internationally. They capture our data, not just preventing us from using it for our own benefit but often undermining our privacy. They are sometimes unreliable and often slow. They exclude 2 billion people who don't have enough money to justify a bank account. Most problematic, they are capturing the benefits of the digital age asymmetrically – and today.

What if there were an Internet of value, a globally distributed, highly secure platform, ledger or database where we could store and exchange value without powerful intermediaries? That's what blockchain technology offers us. Collective self-interest, hard-coded into this new native digital medium for value, ensures the safety, reliability and trustworthiness of commerce online. That's why we call it the Trust Protocol. It presents countless opportunities to blow centralized models to bits – models like the corporation, a pillar of modern capitalism, along with its management canon.

It turns out every business, institution, government and individual can benefit in profound ways. With the rise of a global peer-to-peer platform for identity, trust, reputation and transactions, CEOs will be able to re-engineer deep structures of the firm, for innovation and shared value creation. We're talking about building twenty-first-century companies that look more like networks rather than the vertically integrated hierarchies of the industrial age. CEOs in the financial services industry know that blockchain provides an historic threat and opportunity, and executives in other industries will soon follow.

New business models are emerging everywhere. The 'disruptors' like Uber and AirBnb, may well be disrupted themselves. Most so-called sharing economy companies are really service aggregators. They aggregate the willingness of suppliers to sell their excess capacity (cars, equipment, vacant rooms, handyman skills) through a centralized platform and then resell them to users, all while collecting valuable data for further commercial exploitation. Blockchain technology provides suppliers of these services a means to collaborate, which delivers a greater share of the value to them. Just about everything Uber does could be done by smart agents on a blockchain. The blockchain's trust protocol allows for cooperatives, or autonomous associations, to be formed and controlled by people who come together to meet common needs. All revenues for services, except for overhead, would go to members, who also control the platform and make decisions.

As firms become more like networks, management will change too and smart CEOs will lead this change. How do you effectively manage talent outside your boundaries? Triple entry accounting will eliminate the audit function and enable first to have real-time accounting. Does your CFO understand that? Supply chains will be based on blockchains. Customers will scan your products to find the blockchain-enabled providence of everything you make.

Blockchain may eliminate many of the biggest problems of management. The Distributed Autonomous Organization launched in 2016 had no employees at all. It was smart software based on the Ethereum blockchain. This DAO raised 160 million in a crowdfunding campaign. The problem of 'moral hazard' was eliminated because the software specified that the organization was forced to act in the interests of its shareholders. The grand experiment ultimately failed due to a flaw in its smart contract systems, but the lessons are rich.

Increasingly, CEOs understand that business cannot succeed in a world that's failing. Perhaps the biggest opportunity in the Second Era of the Internet is to free us from the grip of a troubling prosperity paradox. The economy is growing but fewer people are benefiting. This problem is behind the social unrest, extremism, populism, demagoguery and worse – from Brexit to Donald Trump – that is plaguing modern economies. Rather than trying to solve the problem of growing social inequality through redistribution alone, we can change the way wealth – and opportunity – is *pre*distributed in the first place, as people everywhere, from farmers to musicians, can use this technology to share more fully in the wealth they create.

The most important challenge facing the CEO in the mid-1990s was the early Internet. Once again the technology genie has escaped from the bottle, this time with bigger force and implications. Are you preparing your company?

Don Tapscott

Don Tapscott is the author of a number of bestselling books. They include *Paradigm Shift* (1992); *The Digital Economy* (1996); *Growing Up Digital* (1998); *Digital Capital* (2000); *The Naked Corporation* (2003); *Grown Up Digital* (2008); and *The Blockchain Revolution* (2016). He is a Thinkers50 ranked thinker.

From Dave Ulrich

Dear CEO,

First, a note of thanks. You have earned the right to take on a very tough role. CEOs face unprecedented transparency where your public and private moves are visible and discussed in social media. You also face an incredible pace of change and uncertainty where it is difficult to predict the future from the past. This scrutiny and change have kept many from assuming the burdens of being CEO. So, thanks for being able and willing to accept these challenges.

Second, some professional counsel. We (and others) have found in our research that effective leaders are 'paradox navigators' which means that you have to find the right way to balance competing demands. We, along with others, have created 'checklists' for leadership which oversimplify the challenges you face. What we now find is that leaders face a number of paradoxes or tensions that have to be navigated to help your business win, including:

- Being able to zoom out and envision an inspiring future different from the present and being able to zoom in and make daily choices that fold the future into the present;
- Honouring the past which includes your company's heritage and the choices made by your predecessors while creating your future, which means evolving and building on previous agendas as you set your own;

- Leading from the front as you make decisions and act as an example of what you hope your company can become and leading from behind as you build the next generation of leaders who will someday replace you and sustain the company;
- Anticipating customers so that you can serve them what they don't even yet know that they need and engaging employees so that their success is tied to customer success;
- Coordinating and controlling work through clear expectations and discipline (management by objectives) yet allowing employees freedom to make choices and be personally accountable (management by mindset);
- Helping your employees find personal meaning and purpose from their work, yet creating a team or organization that is better than the individuals (our recent research shows that organization has four times the impact on business performance than individual talent);
- And so forth …

To navigate these paradoxes, make sure to surround yourself with people who are both different and, in many ways, better than you. Encourage their openness and dialogue. Diverge often to see other views. But, then converge and be willing to make a decision and move forward at the speed of your industry.

Third, some personal counsel. As noted, being CEO (or other senior leader) today is an incredibly demanding and daunting task. Successfully leading others is not just about managing the above paradoxes around strategy, organization, talent and customers, but requires taking care of yourself. So, here are some reminders which sometimes get lost in the press of business.

Preserve your emotional well-being and be comfortable with who you are by savouring joy in the daily routines of work and life, focusing on what is right more than what is wrong, being absorbed in the 'flow' of an activity and living according your deepest values. Your well-being and attitude infect others.

Cultivate networks by surrounding yourself with great people. Building good networks means making and responding to bids from others, celebrating successes of others, serving others with deliberate acts of kindness, being willing and able to apologize and move on and taking time to be with those who matter most to you.

Develop learning agility by being curious and seeking out new ideas, getting out of your comfort zone with people and ideas, and being willing to fail and then learn from the failure by running into it. Experiment and vary routines so that you avoid ruts.

Find meaning and purpose in the work you do and help others find their meaning from working with you and within your organization. This meaning may come from teammate relationships inside your organization, from customers using your products and services, or from creating an organization culture based on positive values.

So, congratulations on your CEO role: thanks for taking the assignment; navigate the treacherous paradoxes of success; and take care of yourself.

Dave Ulrich

Dave Ulrich is a professor at the Ross School of Business, University of Michigan, and a partner at The RBL Group, a consulting firm. His books – twenty-five at the last count – include *Leadership Sustainability; HR from the Outside-In; The Why of Work; The Leadership Code*; and *Leadership Brand*. He is a Thinkers50 ranked thinker who was shortlisted for the 2015 Breakthrough Idea Award for his concept of 'leadership capital'.

From Liz Wiseman

Dear CEO,

Most companies are adept at hiring smart, talented people but fewer companies actually understand how fully they're using the talent they have acquired. They are fighting a war for talent, but they aren't going to war with their full arsenal of talent.

There is latent intelligence inside most companies – more intellect is 'badging in' the office each morning than is actually getting used. My research has shown that, on average, managers are utilizing only 66 per cent of their people's available capability. In other words, managers are paying a dollar for their resources but only extract 66 cents in capability – a 34 per cent waste. Many managers, hyper-focused on their own ideas and capability, shut down intelligence around them. These diminishing leaders used only 48 per cent of people's intellectual capability. Yet other leaders, whom I call 'multipliers', seem to amplify intelligence around them. These multipliers used 95 per cent, or twice that of the diminishing leaders.

Yet, the costs of underutilized employees are far deeper than simply the waste of payroll dollars. People who are underutilized by their managers described their experience as 'frustrating' and 'exhausting'. Inevitably, the most talented employees quit, creating an expensive turnover problem. The less confident staff often 'quit-and-stay' leaving a more destructive morale problem as disillusioned employees infect the culture.

You probably know how fully staffed your organization is but do you know how fully you are using the intelligence of your staff? Do you have diminishing leaders who are causing people to hold back, play it safe and waste away? As your company grows, the CEO must answer a fundamental question about the role of leadership: Do you expect your managers to have the answers and solve the problem? Or, do you expect them to ask the right questions – the questions that focus the intelligence and energy of their employees on the most crucial problems? The first role is that of the genius. The second is the genius maker, and, right now, it's the genius maker that sits at the top of the intelligence hierarchy.

Smart executives understand that just hiring smart people isn't enough. They need to ensure that managers are harvesting this intelligence and have systems to measure how effectively intelligence is being used in their business. For example, Rajani Ramanathan, the COO of the products and technology division at Salesforce.com, and I measured the depth to which her managers were tapping into the intelligence and capability of their teams. We found they were using an estimated 70 per cent. She challenged her management team to raise this metric by 10 per cent, with hopes to grow both the business and her people. One year later, we re-measured and discovered that the managers in the study collectively raised their score from 70 to 78 per cent. She calculated that, based on the size of her organization, this 11 per cent gain was the rough equivalent of a headcount increase of twenty-five people.

While intelligence use can be measured, it isn't static. There is a growing body of evidence that suggests that human intelligence is extensible – it actually grows with use, and, conversely, shrinks from neglect. Consider other research that shows how managers can grow the intelligence of their teams by keeping their staff in hyper-learning mode.

When employees work in their areas of expertise, they tend to draw on best practices and play it safe, both highly useful in times of stability. However, we find that when we are new to something – whether we are 25 or 65 years old – a learner's advantage kicks in. In the process of asking and experimenting, we tend to do our best thinking, often outperforming those with experience – especially in speed and innovation, both critical in times of rapid change.

We also found that as employees report higher levels of challenge in their work, they also report higher levels of satisfaction. Too many managers are shouldering the tough business decisions themselves, leaving their employee to idle away at the quotidian tasks. Want your employees to do their best work? If so, keep them working on the outer fringe of their capability. Instead of passing out annual goals, managers should feed their team a steady diet of challenge. On average, employees report being ready for a new challenge every three months.

Both in times of growth and scarcity, the wisest executives will look beyond hiring and focus on utilizing their company's existing brainpower. If you want a company that is battle ready, take inventory of your talent and ensure you are using all your firepower. And, if you want a smart, agile organization, make sure your people lead like multipliers and keep thinking like rookies. In a fast-moving environment, it's not what you know that matters, it's how fast you can learn.

Liz Wiseman

A former Oracle executive, **Liz Wiseman** is the author of *Multipliers* (Harper, 2010) and *Rookie Smarts: Why Learning Beats Knowing in the New World of Work* (HarperBusiness, 2014). She is a Thinkers50 ranked thinker.

From Chris Zook

Dear CEO,

The other day you complained about how hard it is – now that your company has grown so much – for you to get things done. You have less time to visit the front line, and even just to think. Most of your calendar for the year ahead is already blocked out for meetings. The 'energy vampires' have taken hold, pursuing their own agendas, sucking away the sense of collective purpose that used to make your company great. You're spending all of your time getting 'alignment' among your staff instead of getting things done. Everything is just more complicated, and this complexity is slowing you down. The result is inevitable: customer loyalty and financial performance are down.

You're not alone. You've fallen prey to the paradox of growth. It's a simple idea: successful growth creates complexity, and complexity kills growth. The paradox can manifest itself in all sorts of ways. To cope with the demands of growth, your leadership team adds layers of management, which means it operates at an increasing remove from the front line. Power shifts to staff departments, often led by people who have never served a customer. Your leaders now lack the ground-level instincts that once made your company so responsive and adaptable. Flush with resources, you move into new areas, but as you do you move away from your core. You're now at risk of becoming … just another company.

This is all natural – and dangerous. Every fifteen years or so, two of every three large and successful companies will collapse under the weight of their own complexity. And in 85 per cent of those cases, they'll do so because of internal, not external, problems.

Fortunately, these problems can be addressed – by restoring the attitudes and behaviours that make up what I call 'the founder's mentality'. It's the founder's mentality what made you successful in the first place, and returning to it as you grow is one of the greatest and most undervalued secrets of business success.

So what does restoring the founder's mentality entail?

First, you have to renew your sense of yourself as an insurgent – as a company that wages war against its industry on behalf of underserved customers, or that redefines the rules of its industry, or that creates new markets. This means addressing fundamental questions about your mission. What truly distinguishes your company? Where do you spike? Consider Nike, which has achieved decades of success and fought off stall-out several times in its history. How has the company managed this? By staying true to its original mission, which was to help athletes perform better. How does Nike spike? By forging relationships with half of the top ten athletes in nearly all of the sports it serves. Focus, focus, focus.

Second, you have to renew the obsession with the front line that made you succeed in the first place. That means making those who work on the front line the heroes of your organization. The hotel company Oberoi stands at the top of its industry because it gives its employees the power and incentives to solve customer problems on the spot. This strategy is critical. Employees who connected and empowered in this way are five times more likely to invest their own time to solve problems and generate innovative ideas.

Third, you have to return to an owner's mindset. This means becoming a meritocracy again: a place where employees take responsibility rather than avoiding it, and make speed rather than inaction their bias. If your staff don't prioritize these things – if they don't make every decision as if the company they work for is their own – your company will gradually devolve into a bureaucracy. And bureaucracies always lose to fast, young insurgents (like you once were).

During the past decade, only about one company in ten achieved more than a modest level of sustained and profitable growth. That's a sobering statistic, but here's the good news: companies that evince the traits of the founder's mentality are five times more likely to perform in the top quartile than the rest. How did struggling companies such as Starbuck's, Disney, Home Depot and Dell – along with existentially threatened companies such as Apple, LEGO Group and DaVita – all manage to turn themselves around? By assiduously restoring the traits of the founder's mentality.

You can do the same. Start by asking yourself with a couple of practical questions. What characterized your company when it was at its greatest and most special? What have you lost? Now get personal. What would it take to make your company the kind of place you hoped to work for when you entered the workforce?

Better yet, what would it take to make it the kind of place your children might hope to build their careers?

Chris Zook

Chris Zook is a partner in Bain & Company's Boston office. He is the author of *The Founder's Mentality* (Harvard Business Review Press, 2016). Based on a decade-long study of companies in more than forty countries, *The Founder's Mentality* shows how leaders can overcome the predictable crises of growth and set their companies on a path of sustainable growth. Chris Zook is a Thinkers50 ranked thinker.